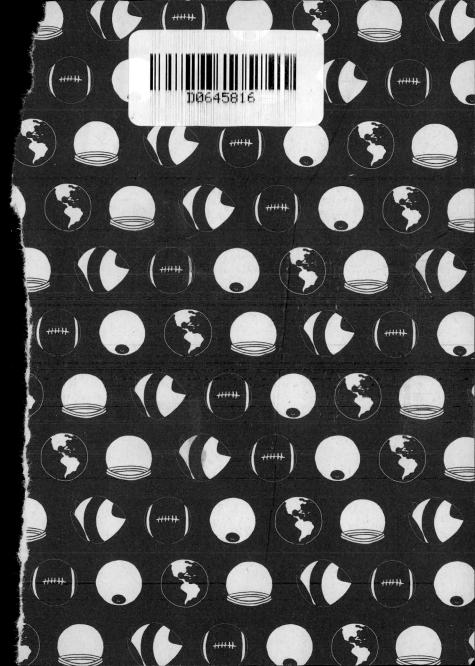

D0645816

XTC69
JESSICA CAMPBELL

WITHDRAWN

KOYAMA PRESS

All work is © 2018 Jessica Campbell
jessicacampbell.biz

All rights reserved. No part of this publication (except small
portions for review purposes) may be reproduced or trans-
mitted in any form without the prior written permission of the
publisher or artist.

Published by Koyama Press
koyamapress.com

First edition: May 2018

ISBN: 978-1-927668-57-3

Printed in Canada

Koyama Press gratefully acknowledges the Canada Council
for the Arts and the Ontario Arts Council for their support of
our publishing program.

DEDICATED TO
ANNA JACQUES AND
MARNIE FORGAY

CHAPTER 1:
PER MARE, PER TERRAS

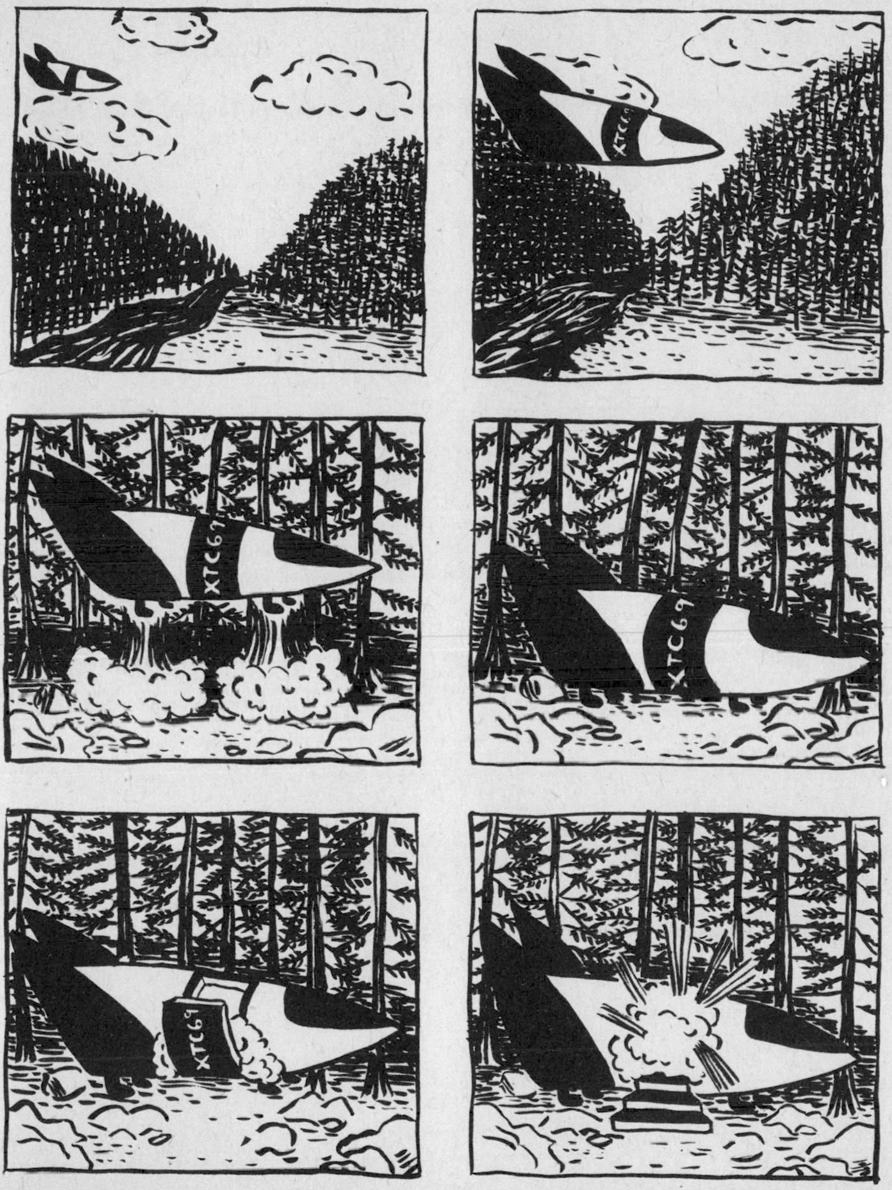
XTC69
XTC69
XTC69

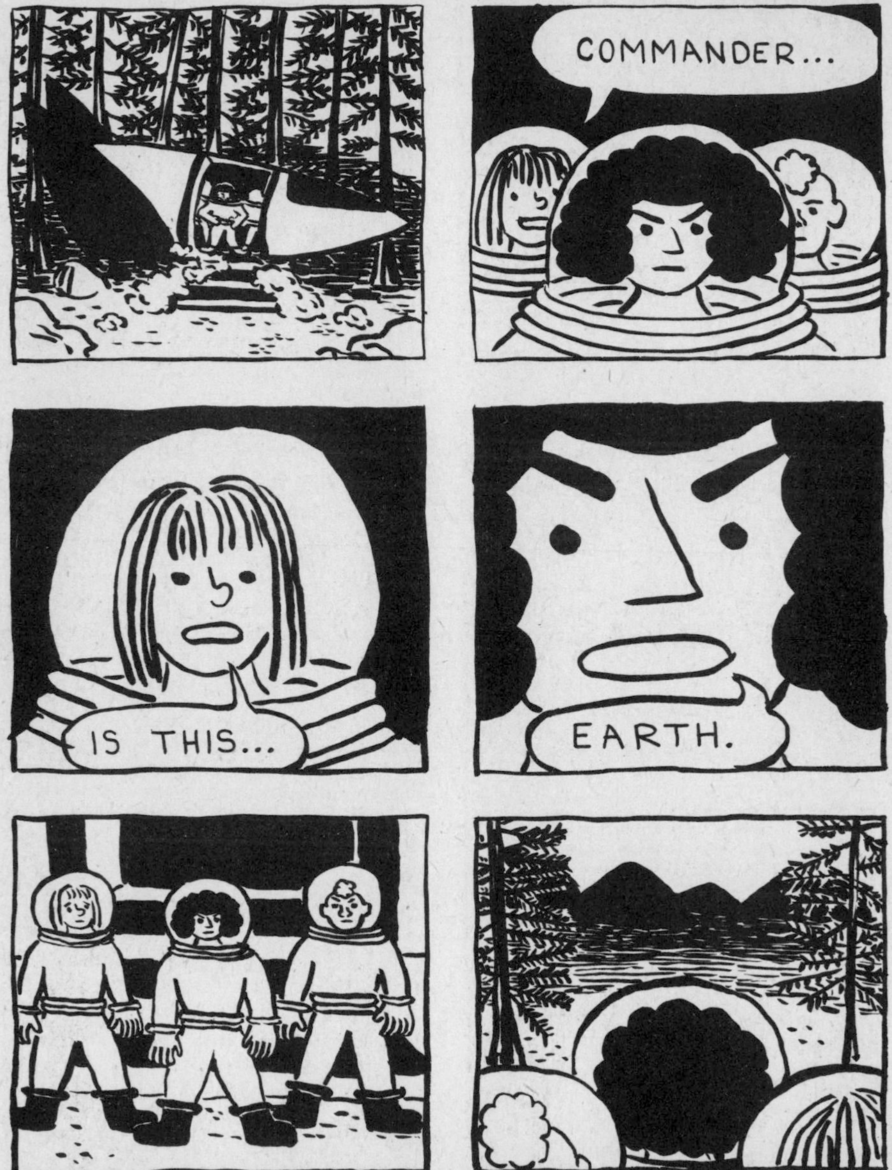
COMMANDER...
IS THIS...
EARTH.

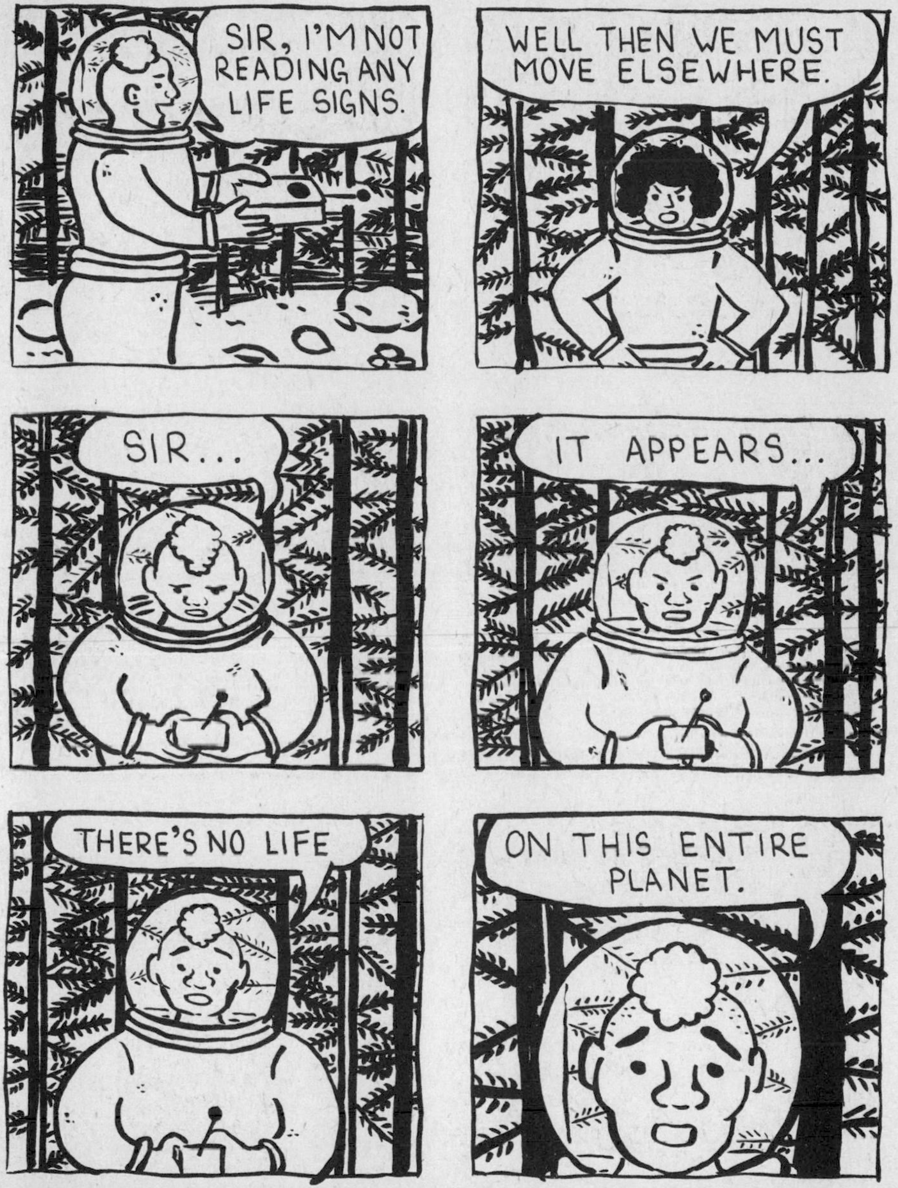
SIR, I'M NOT READING ANY LIFE SIGNS.
WELL THEN WE MUST MOVE ELSEWHERE.
SIR...
IT APPEARS...
THERE'S NO LIFE
ON THIS ENTIRE PLANET.

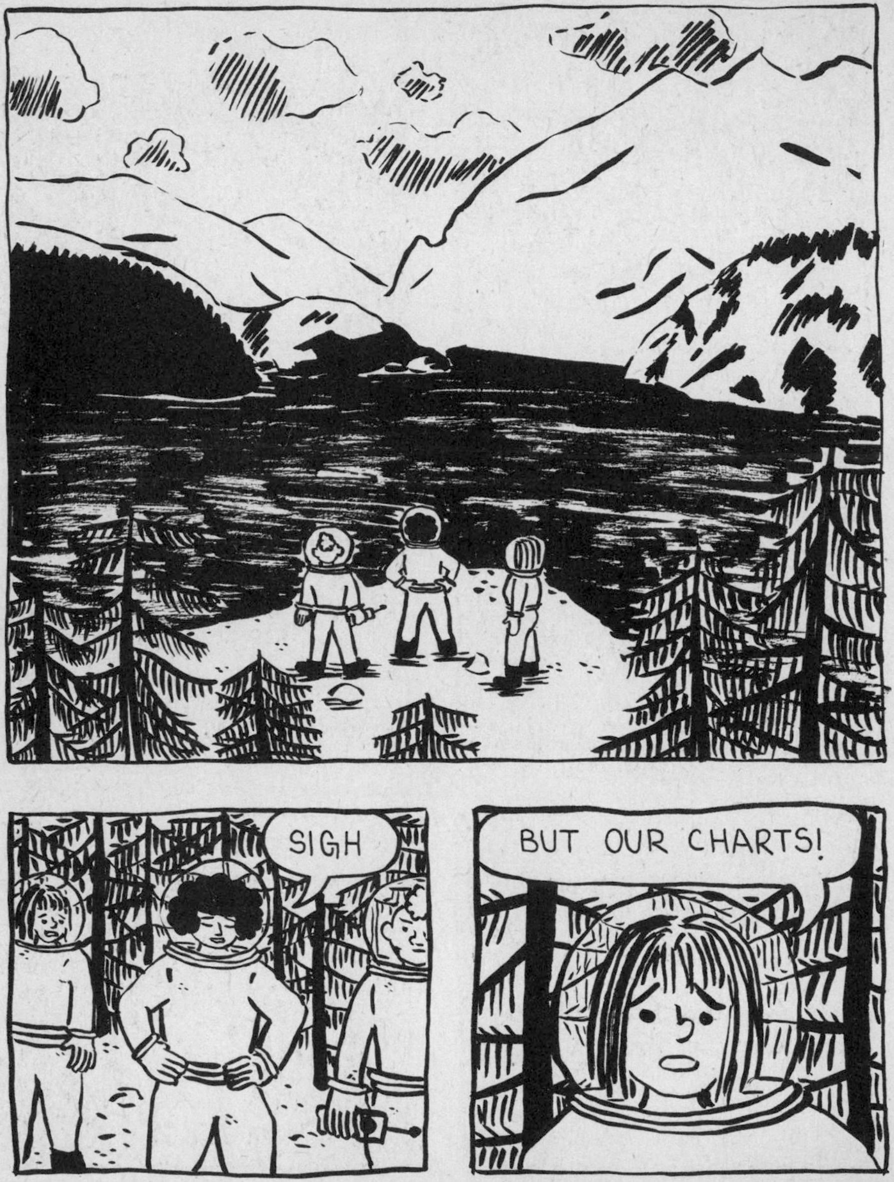
SIGH
BUT OUR CHARTS!

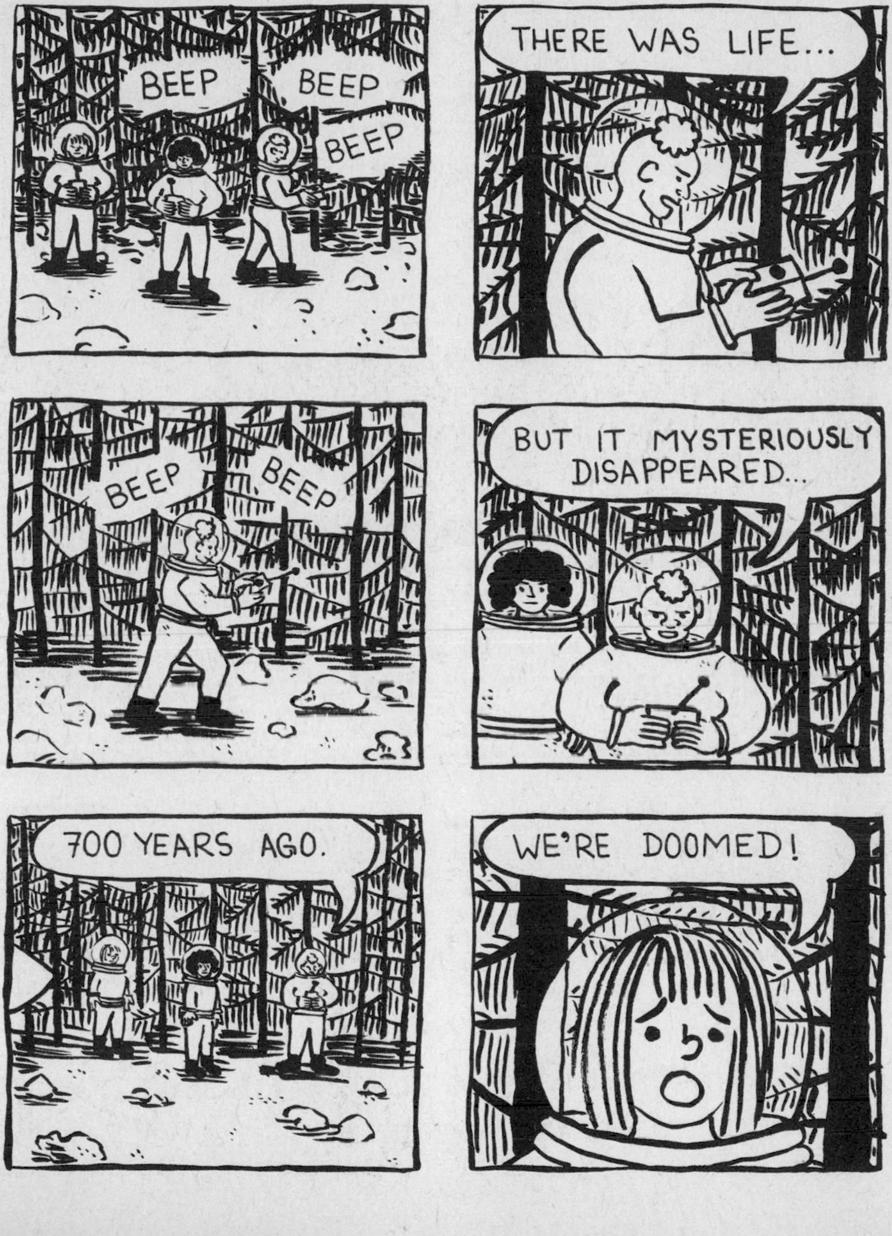
BEEP
BEEP
BEEP
THERE WAS LIFE...
BEEP
BEEP
BUT IT MYSTERIOUSLY DISAPPEARED...
700 YEARS AGO.
WE'RE DOOMED!

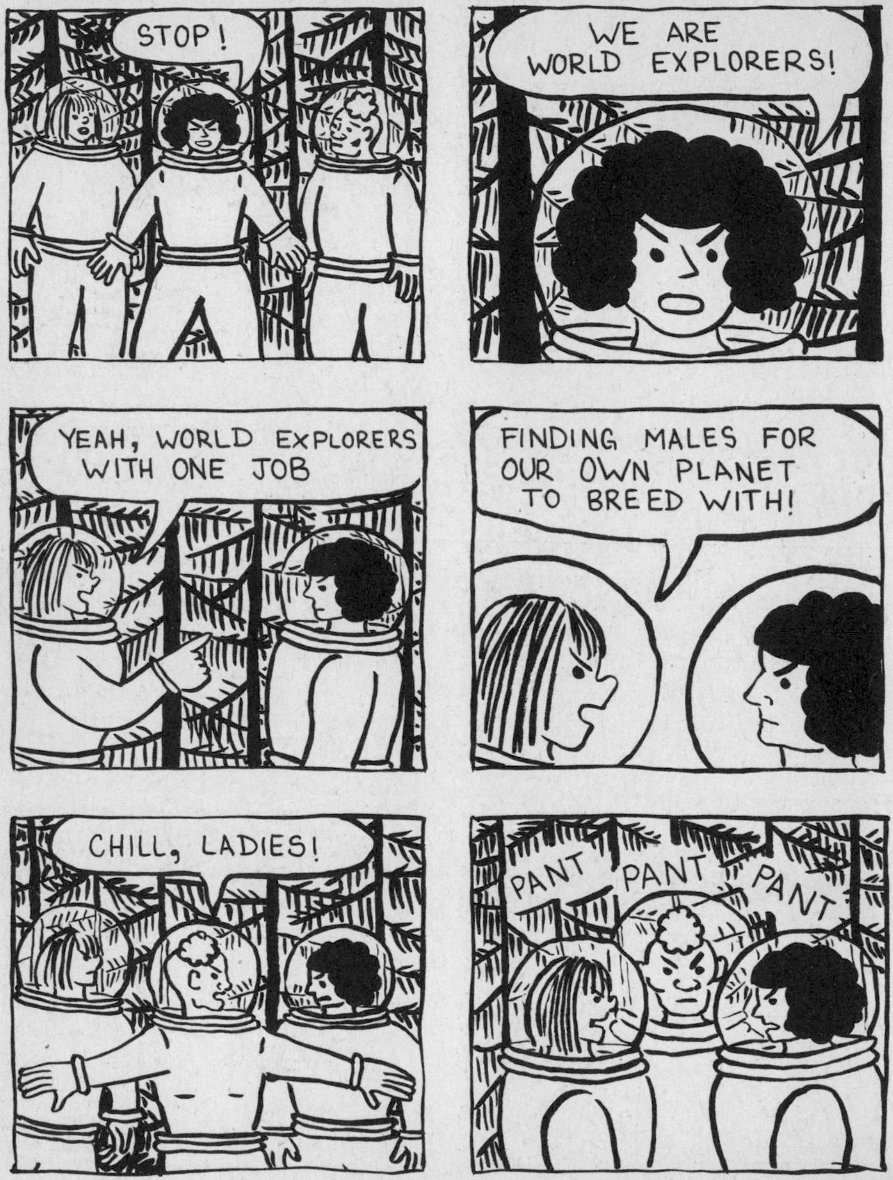
STOP!
WE ARE WORLD EXPLORERS!
YEAH, WORLD EXPLORERS WITH ONE JOB
FINDING MALES FOR OUR OWN PLANET TO BREED WITH!
CHILL, LADIES!
PANT PANT PANT

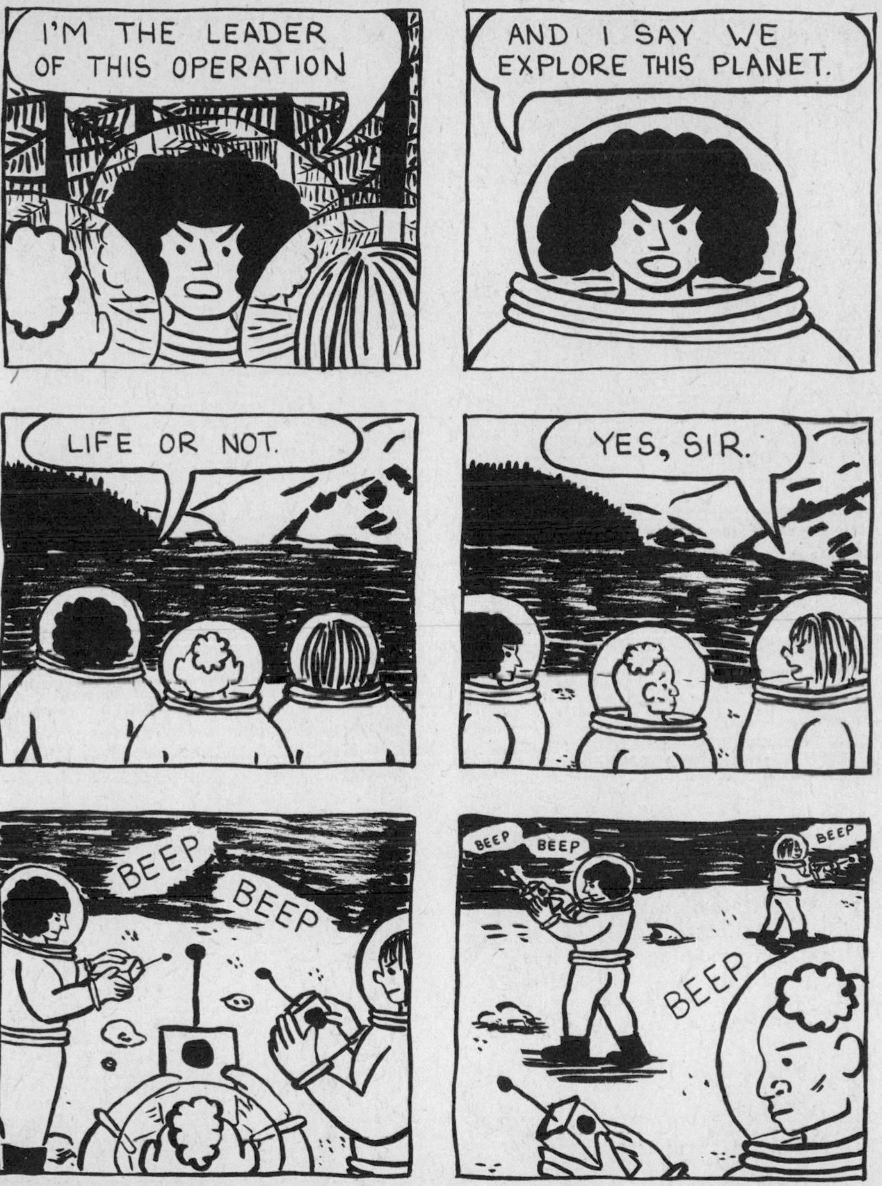
I'M THE LEADER OF THIS OPERATION
AND I SAY WE EXPLORE THIS PLANET.
LIFE OR NOT.
YES, SIR.
BEEP
BEEP
BEEP
BEEP
BEEP
BEEP

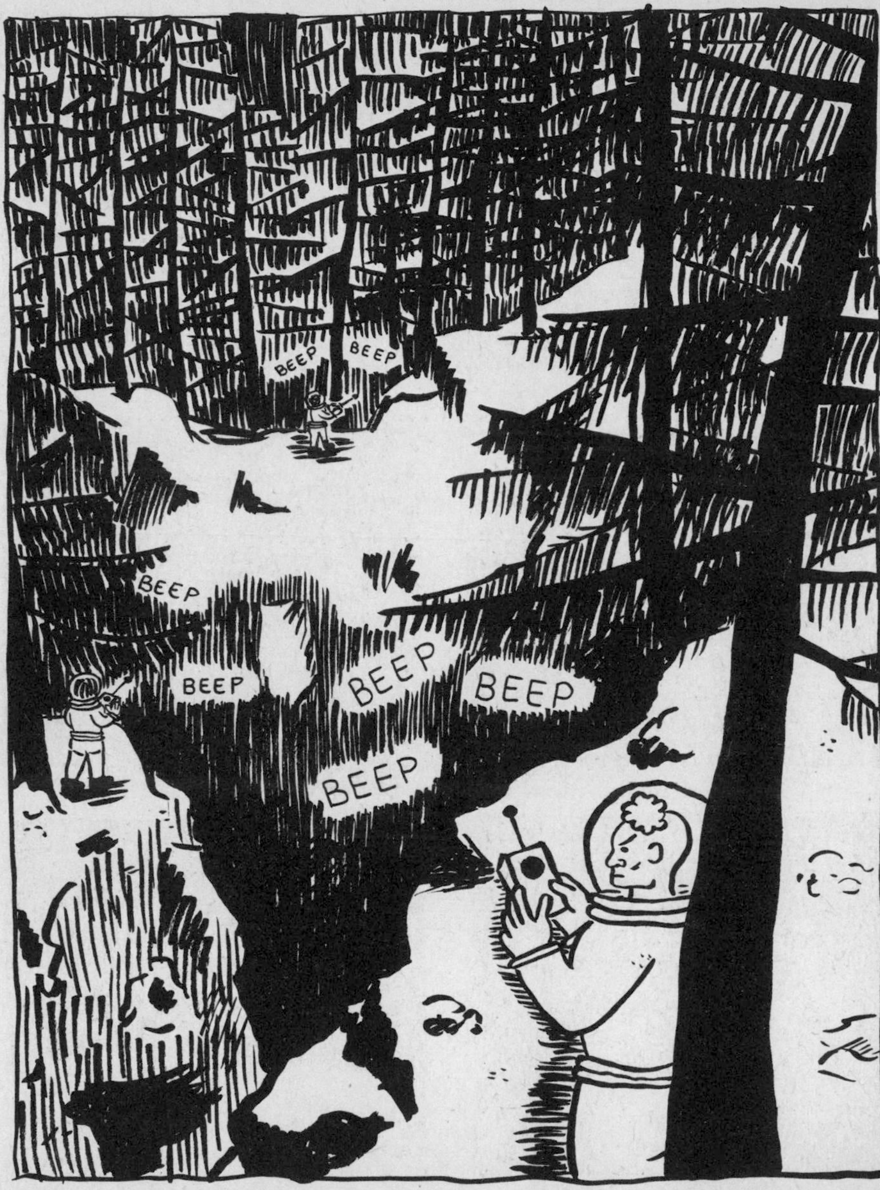
BEEP
BEEP
BEEP
BEEP
BEEP
BEEP
BEEP

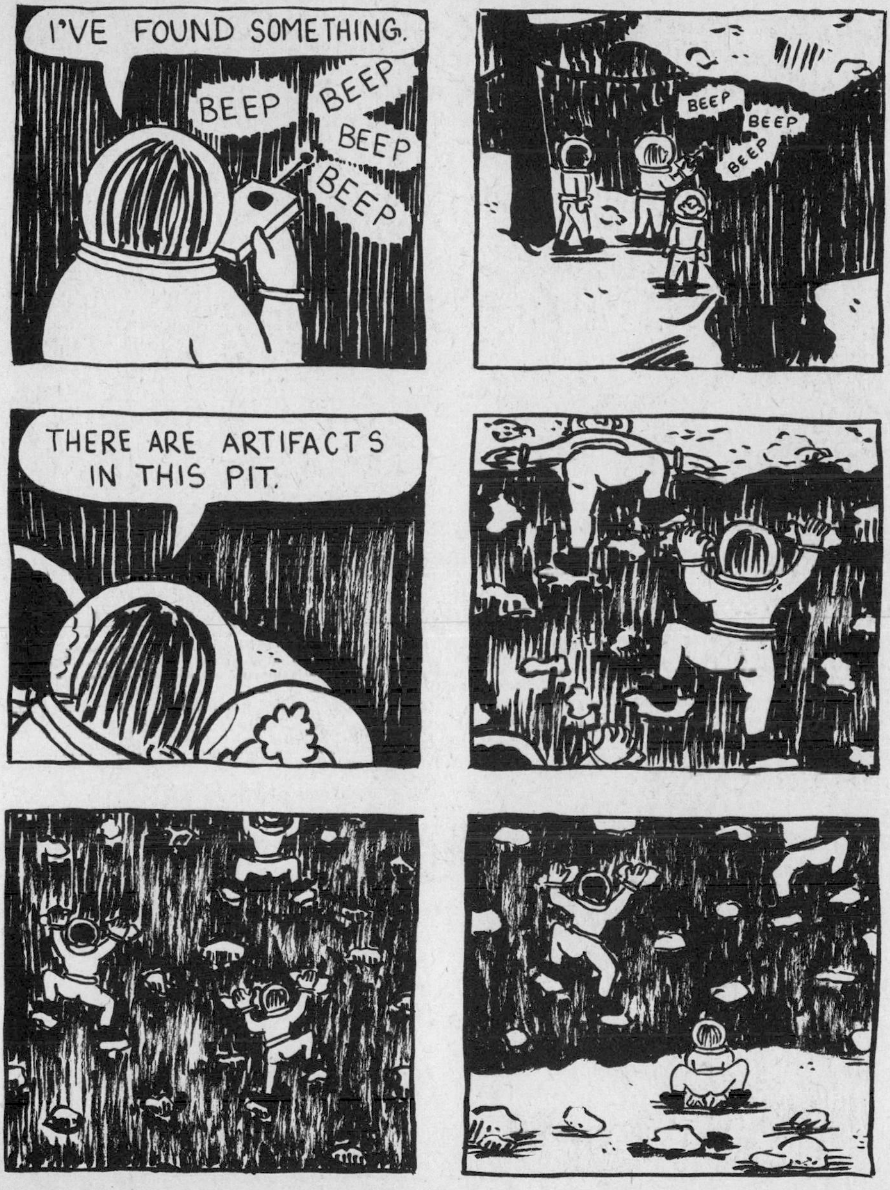
I'VE FOUND SOMETHING.
BEEP
BEEP
BEEP
BEEP
BEEP
BEEP
BEEP
THERE ARE ARTIFACTS IN THIS PIT.

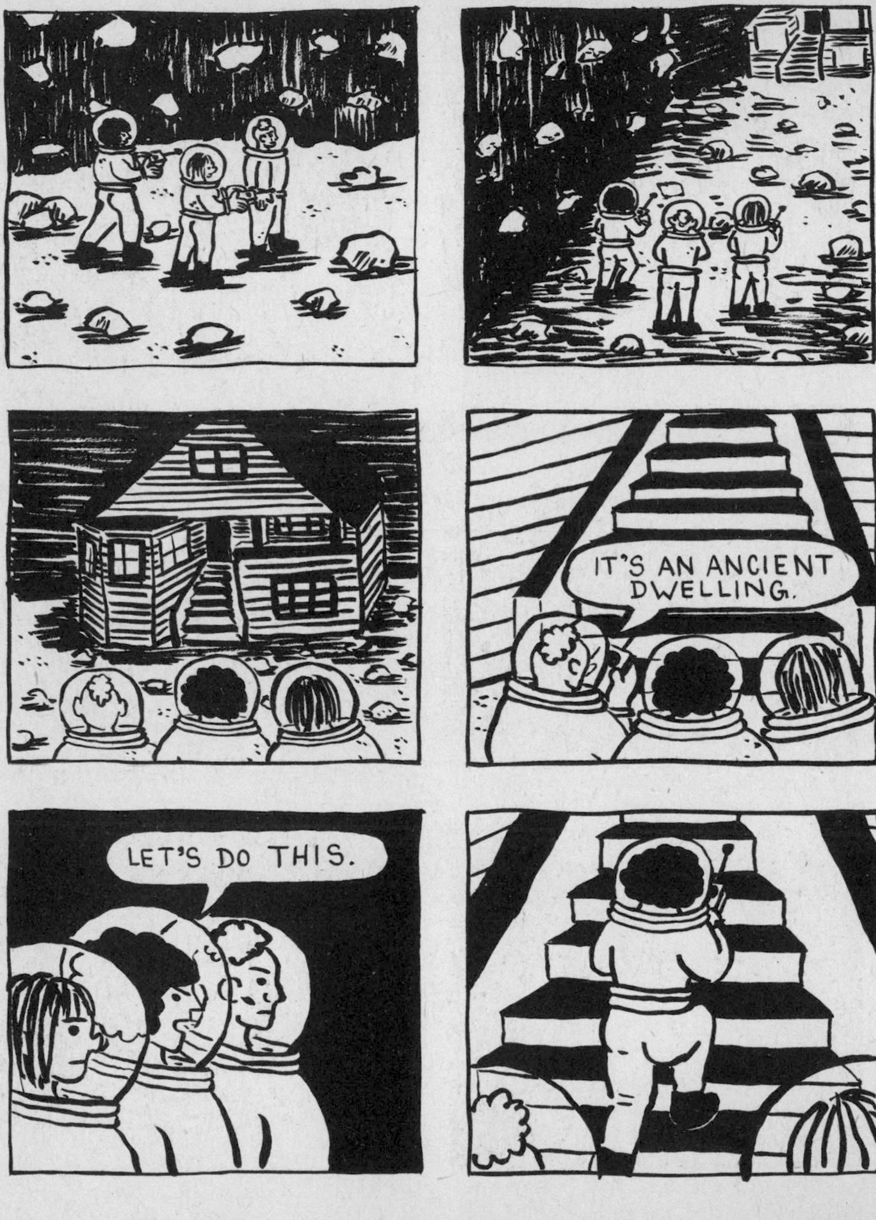
IT'S AN ANCIENT DWELLING.
LET'S DO THIS.

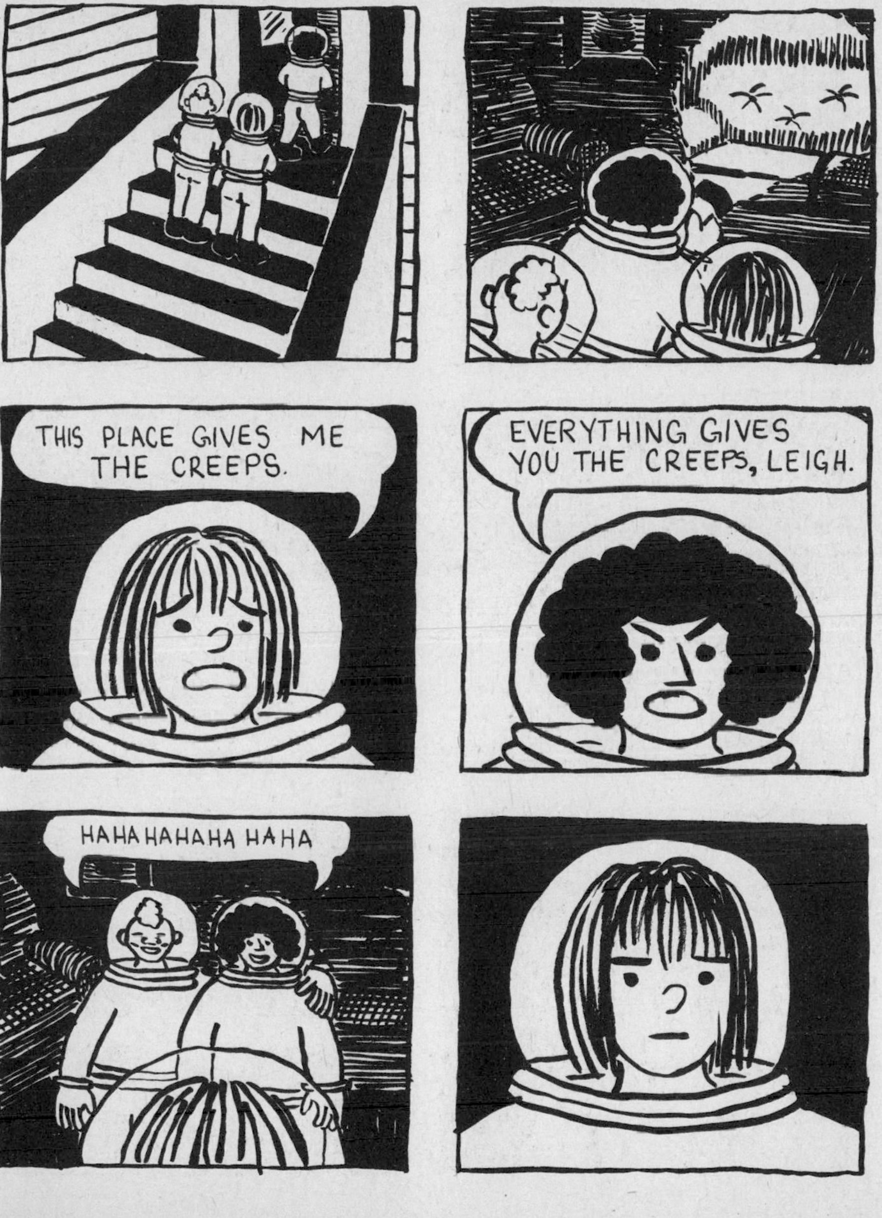
THIS PLACE GIVES ME THE CREEPS.
EVERYTHING GIVES YOU THE CREEPS, LEIGH.
HAHAHAHAHA HAHA

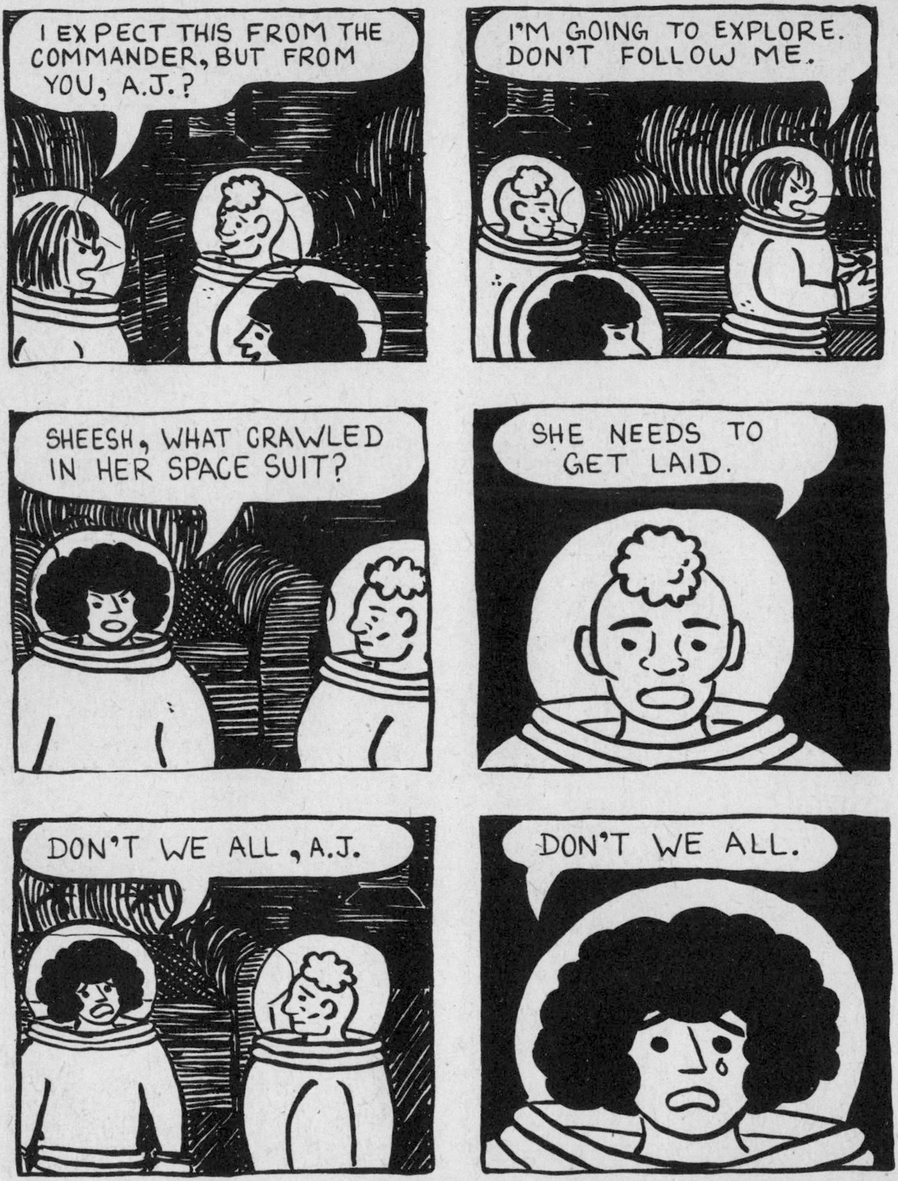
I EXPECT THIS FROM THE COMMANDER, BUT FROM YOU, A.J.?
I'M GOING TO EXPLORE. DON'T FOLLOW ME.
SHEESH, WHAT CRAWLED IN HER SPACE SUIT?
SHE NEEDS TO GET LAID.
DON'T WE ALL, A.J.
DON'T WE ALL.

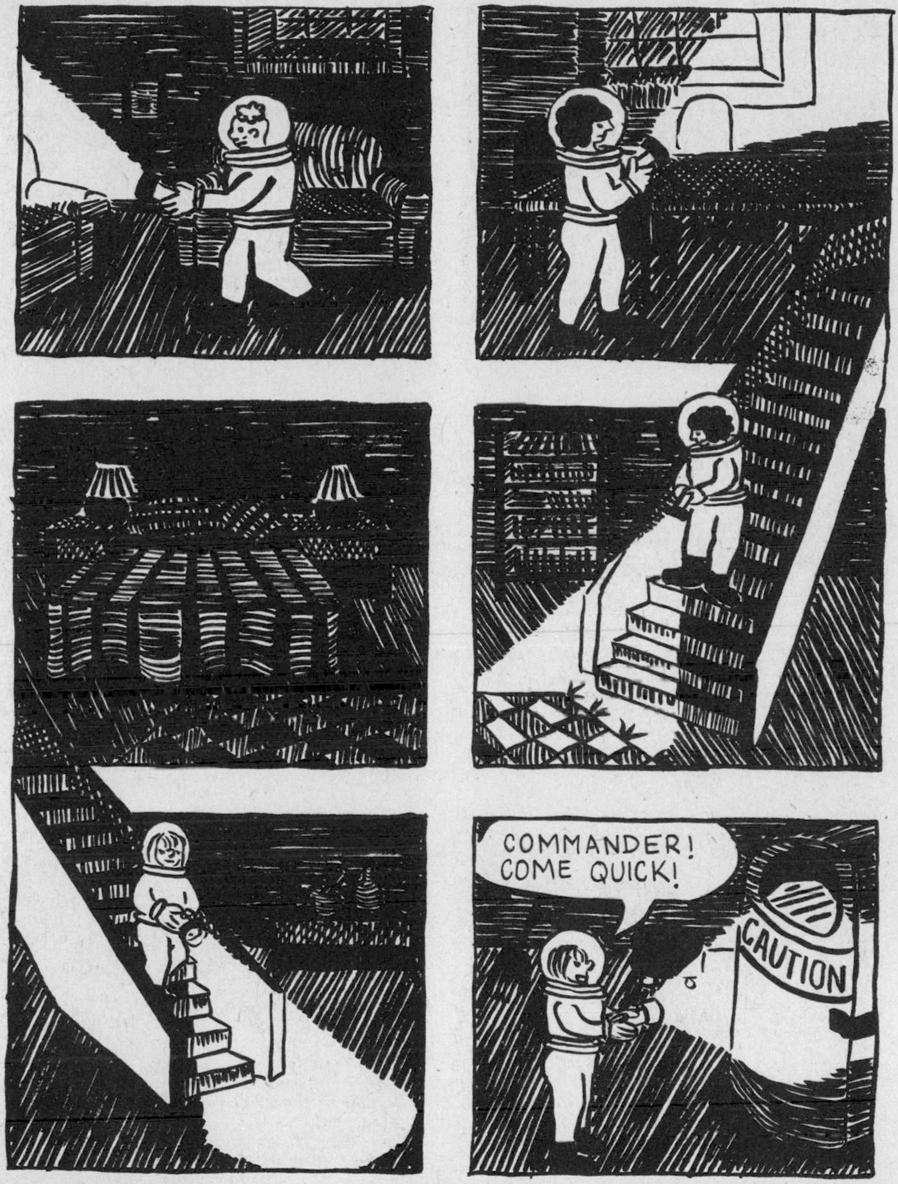
COMMANDER! COME QUICK!
CAUTION

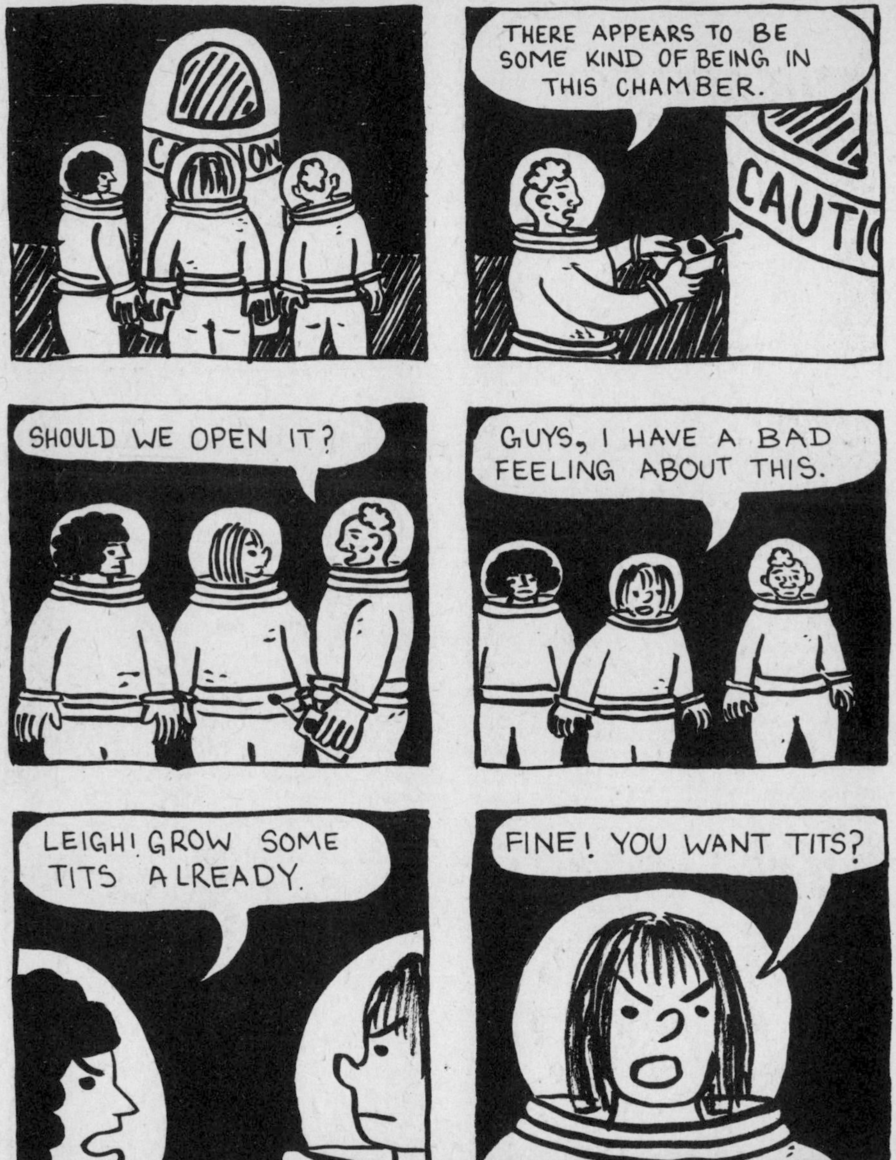
CAUTION
THERE APPEARS TO BE SOME KIND OF BEING IN THIS CHAMBER.
CAUTI
SHOULD WE OPEN IT?
GUYS, I HAVE A BAD FEELING ABOUT THIS.
LEIGH! GROW SOME TITS ALREADY.
FINE! YOU WANT TITS?

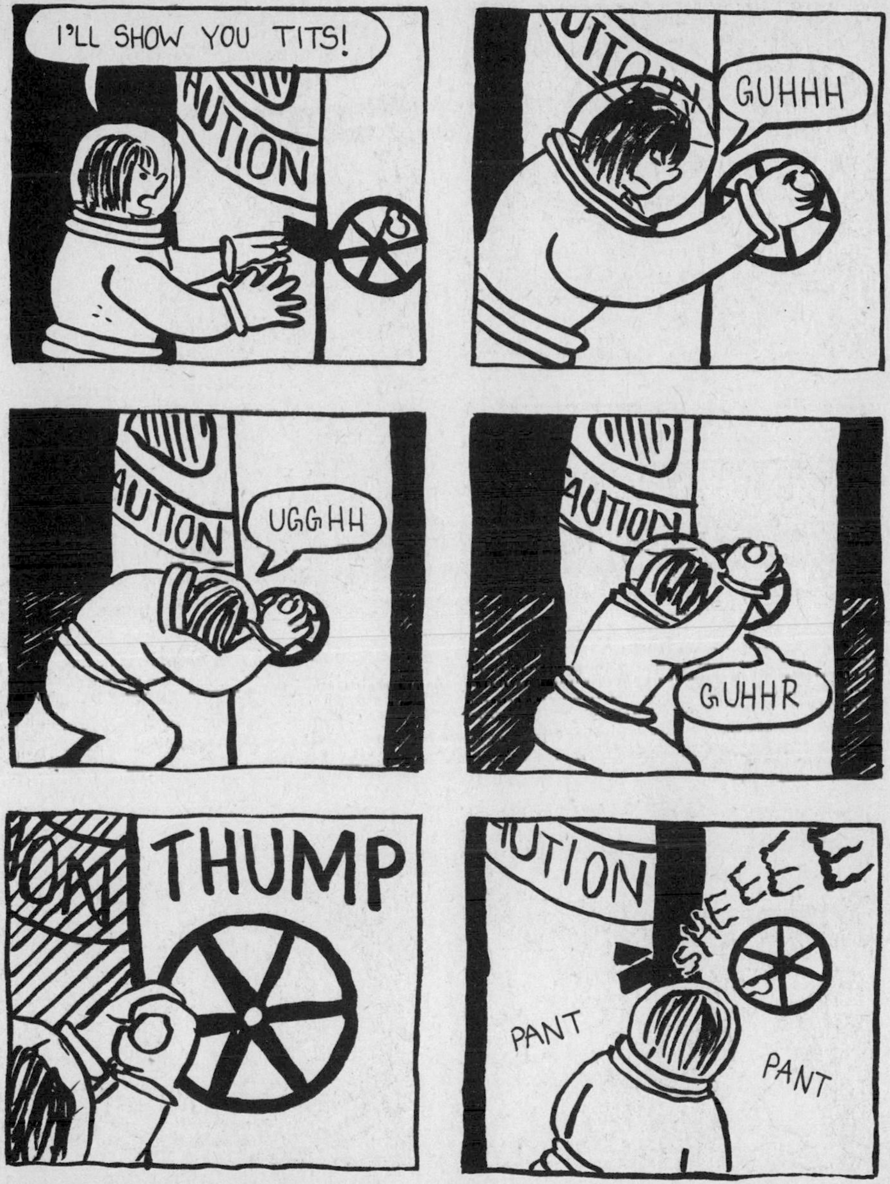
I'LL SHOW YOU TITS!
AUTION
UTION
GUHHH
AUTION
UGGHH
AUTION
GUHHR
ON
THUMP
UTION
SHEEEEE
PANT
PANT

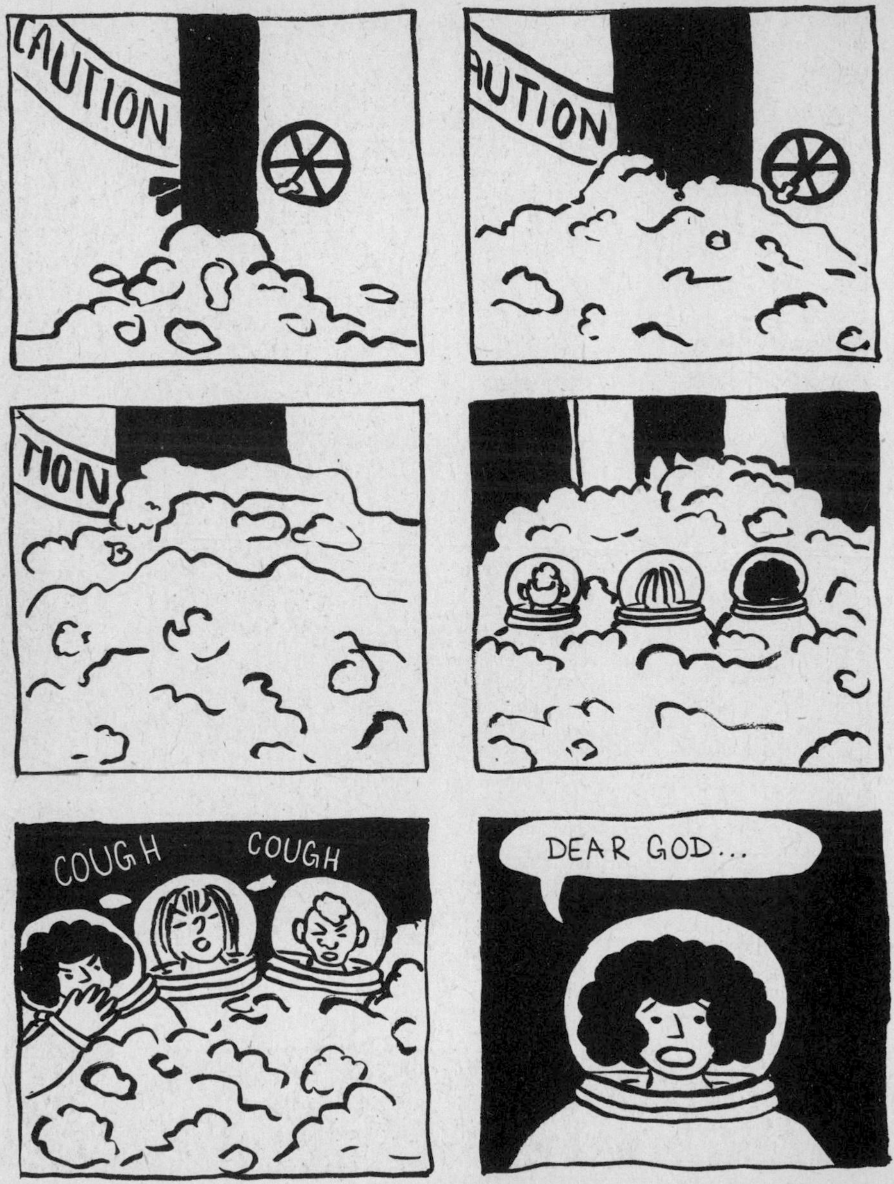
CAUTION
AUTION
TION
COUGH
COUGH
DEAR GOD...

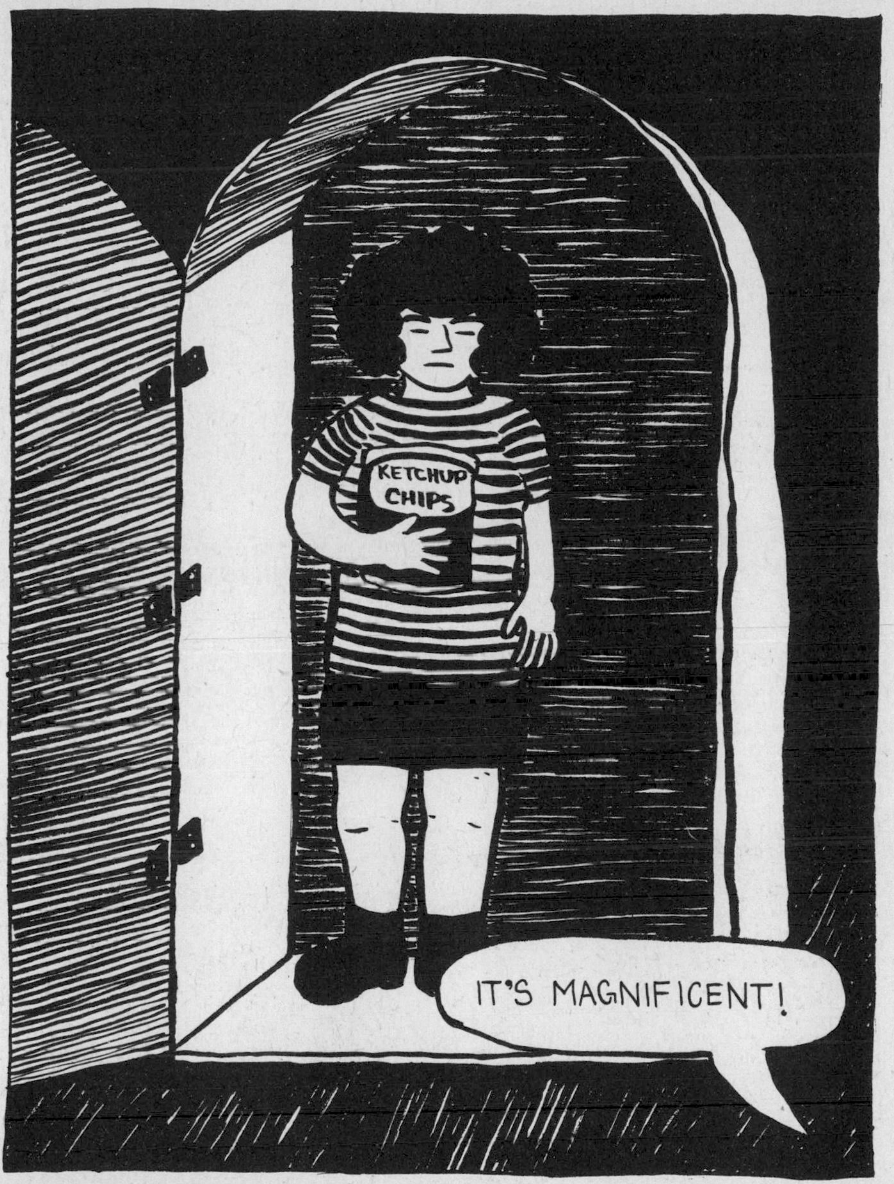
KETCHUP CHIPS
IT'S MAGNIFICENT!

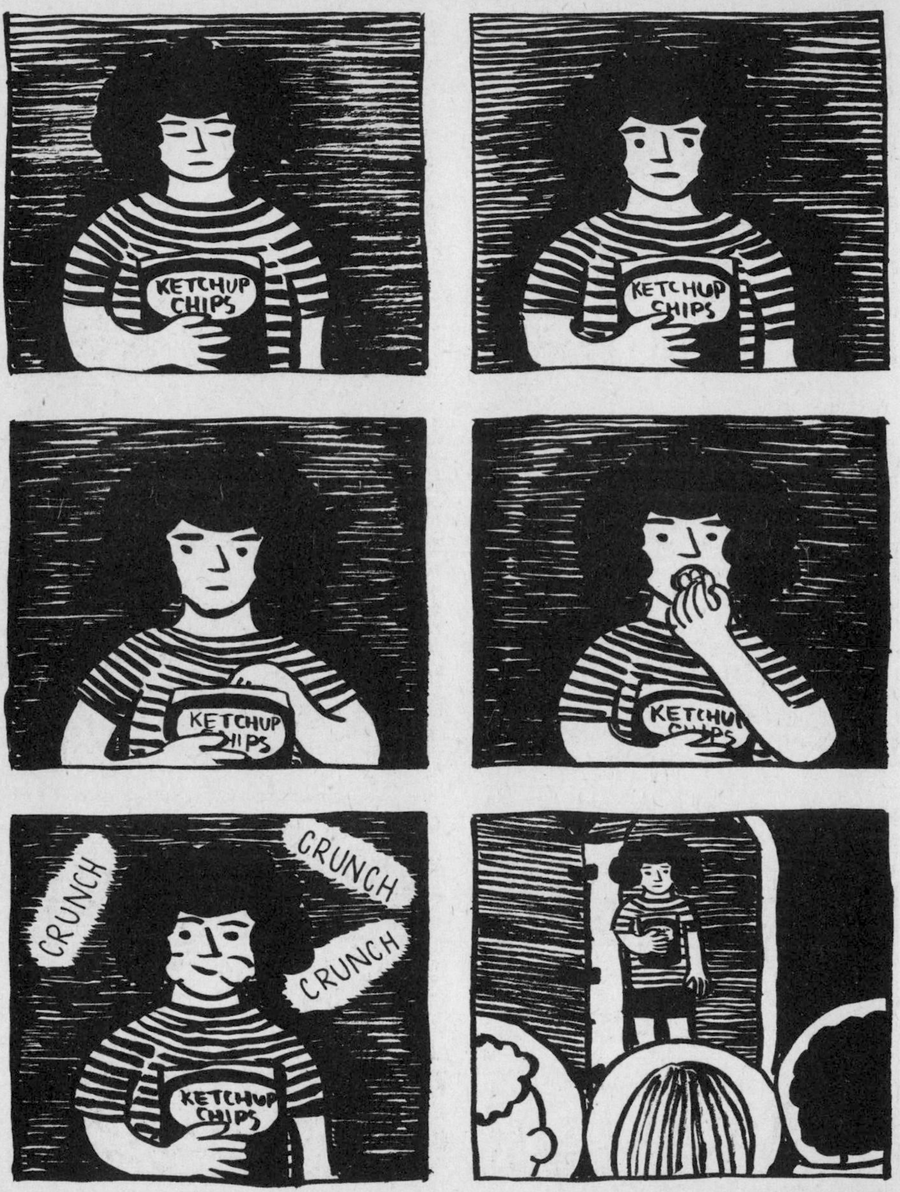
KETCHUP CHIPS
KETCHUP CHIPS
KETCHUP CHIPS
KETCHUP
CRUNCH
CRUNCH
CRUNCH
KETCHUP CHIPS

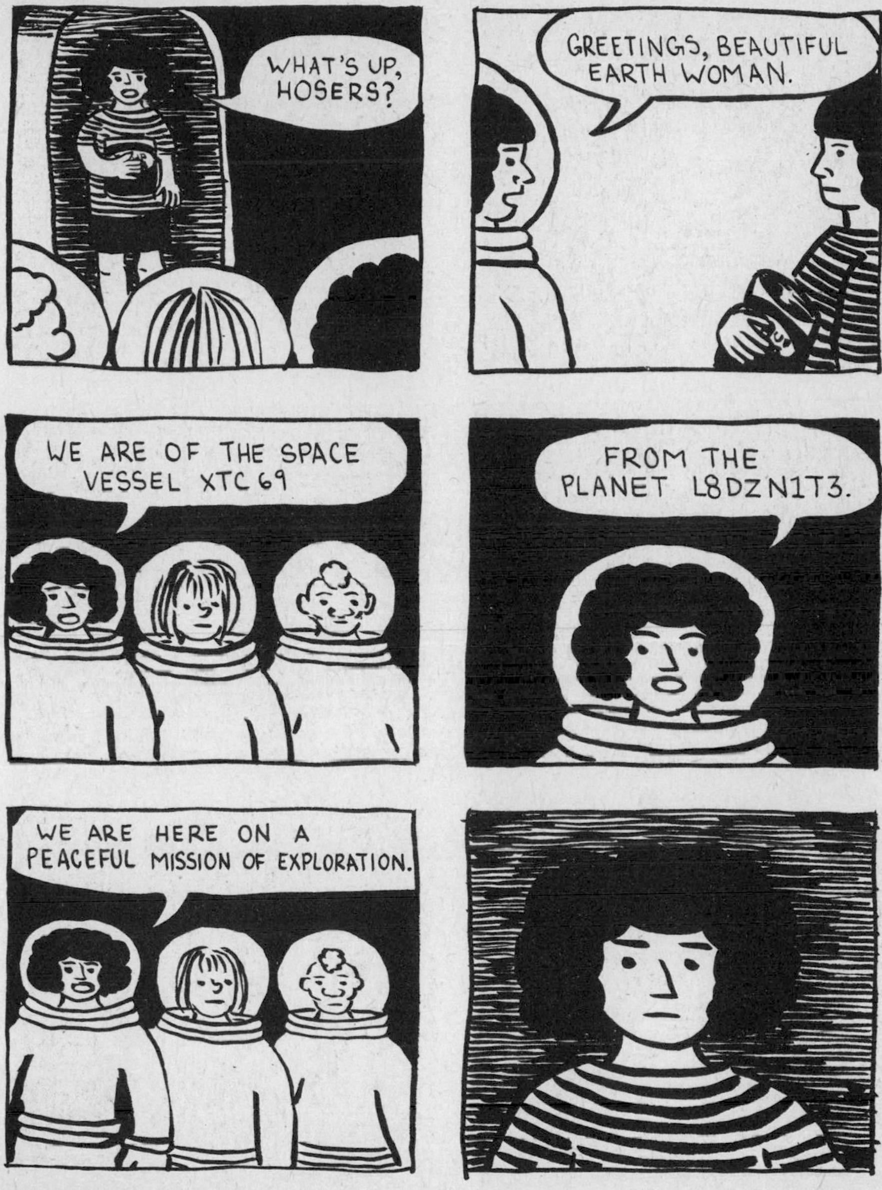
WHAT'S UP, HOSERS?
GREETINGS, BEAUTIFUL EARTH WOMAN.
WE ARE OF THE SPACE VESSEL XTC 69
FROM THE PLANET L8DZN1T3.
WE ARE HERE ON A PEACEFUL MISSION OF EXPLORATION.

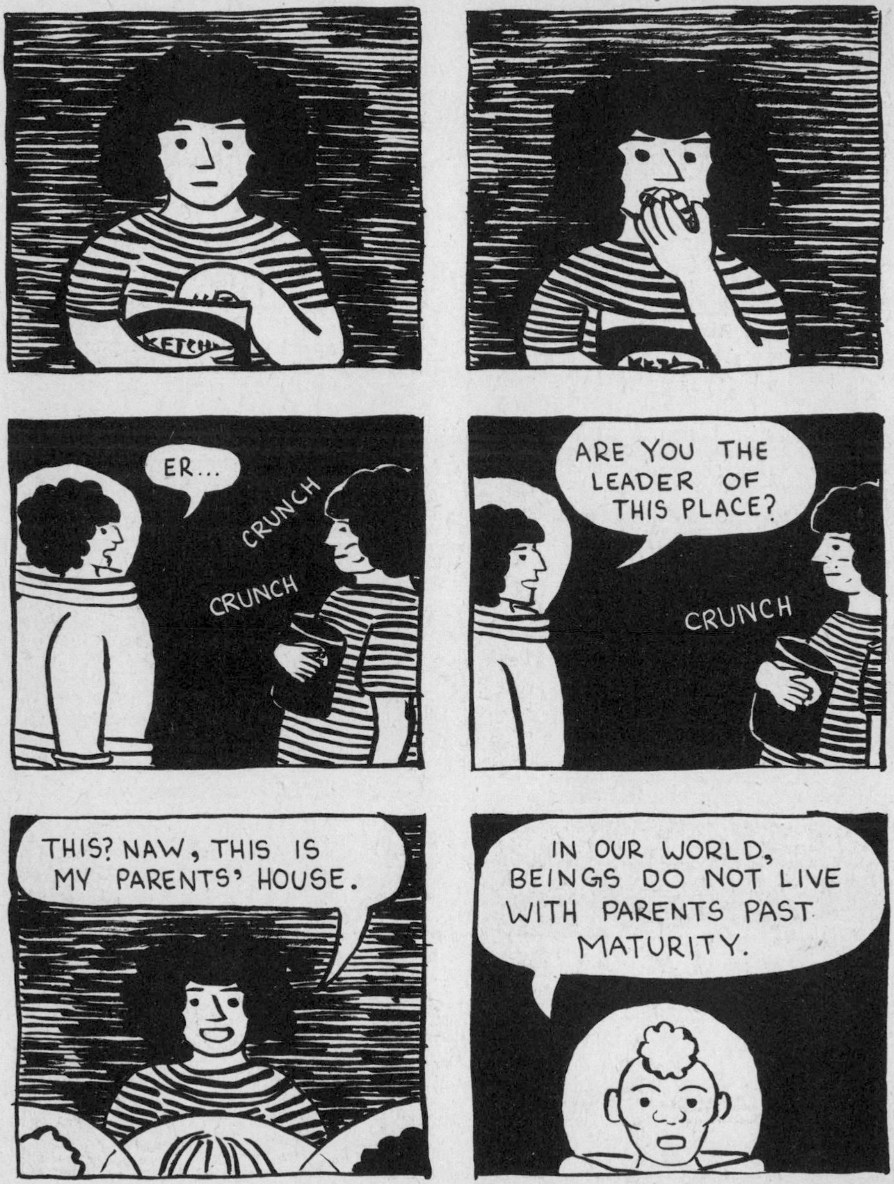
ER...
CRUNCH
CRUNCH
ARE YOU THE LEADER OF THIS PLACE?
CRUNCH
THIS? NAW, THIS IS MY PARENTS' HOUSE.
IN OUR WORLD, BEINGS DO NOT LIVE WITH PARENTS PAST MATURITY.

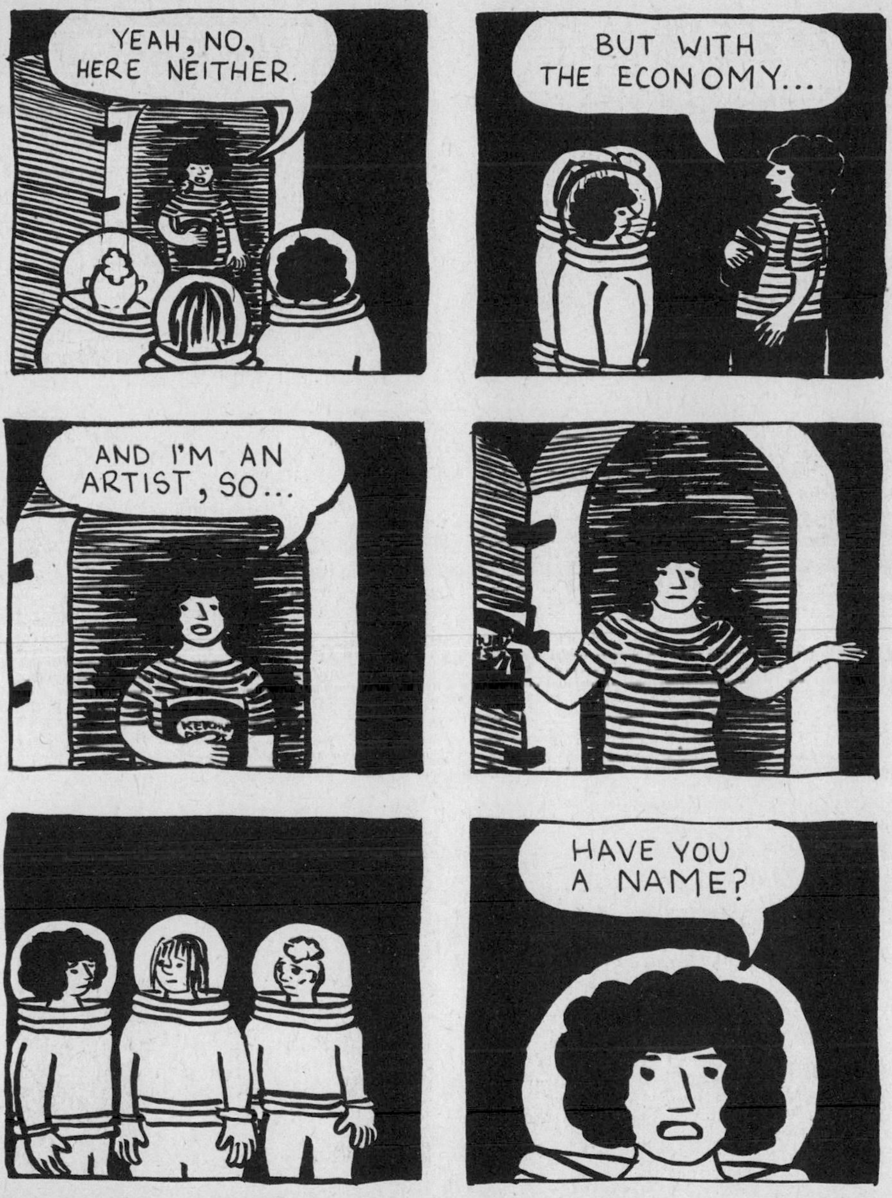
YEAH, NO, HERE NEITHER.
BUT WITH THE ECONOMY...
AND I'M AN ARTIST, SO...
HAVE YOU A NAME?

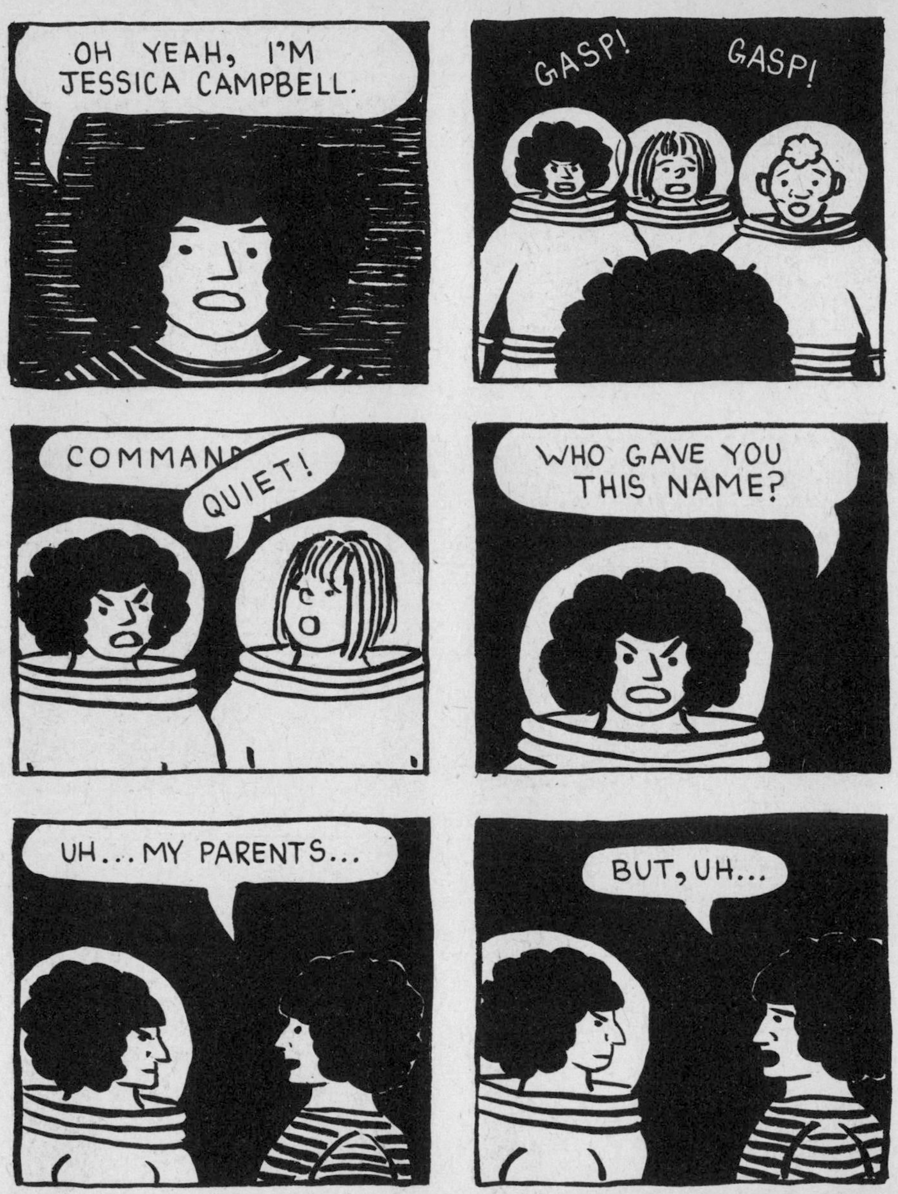
OH YEAH, I'M JESSICA CAMPBELL.
GASP!
GASP!
COMMAN
QUIET!
WHO GAVE YOU THIS NAME?
UH... MY PARENTS...
BUT, UH...

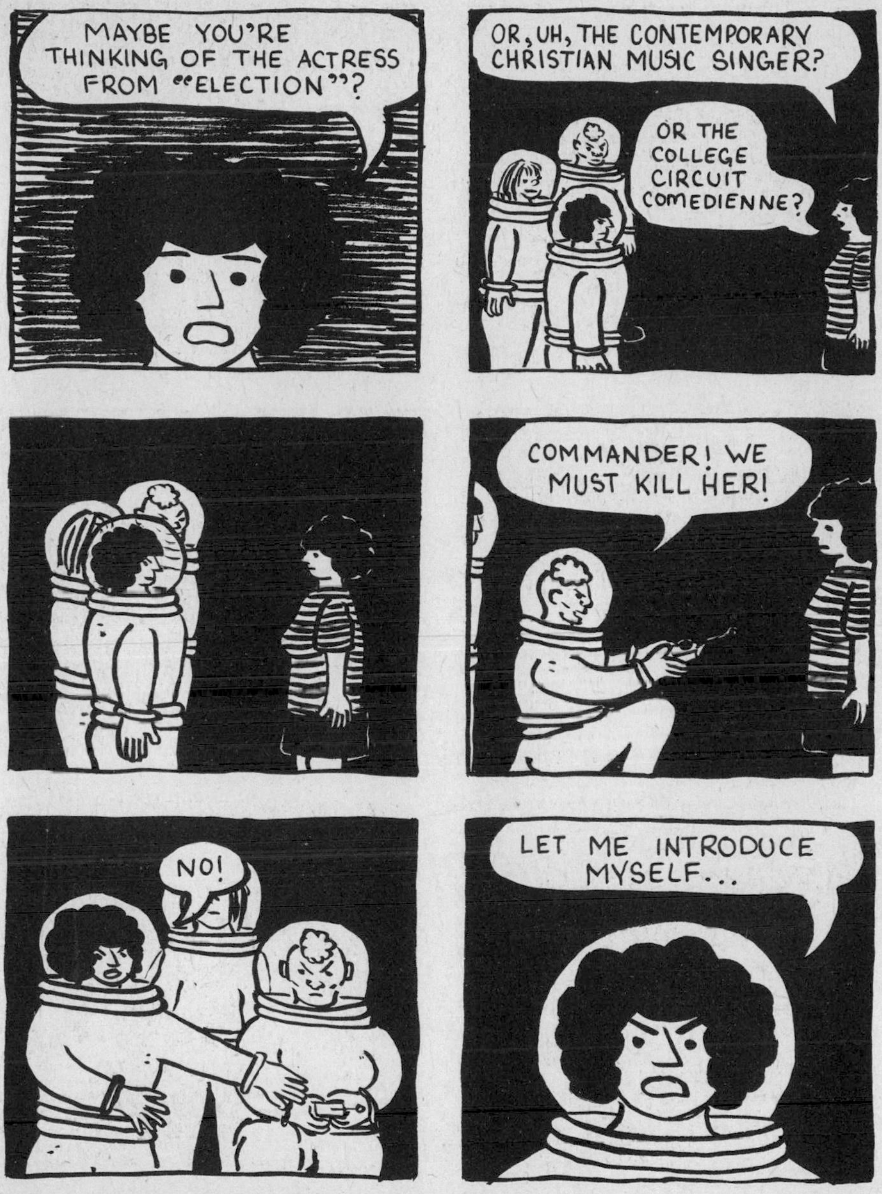
MAYBE YOU'RE THINKING OF THE ACTRESS FROM "ELECTION"?
OR, UH, THE CONTEMPORARY CHRISTIAN MUSIC SINGER?
OR THE COLLEGE CIRCUIT COMEDIENNE?
COMMANDER! WE MUST KILL HER!
NO!
LET ME INTRODUCE MYSELF...

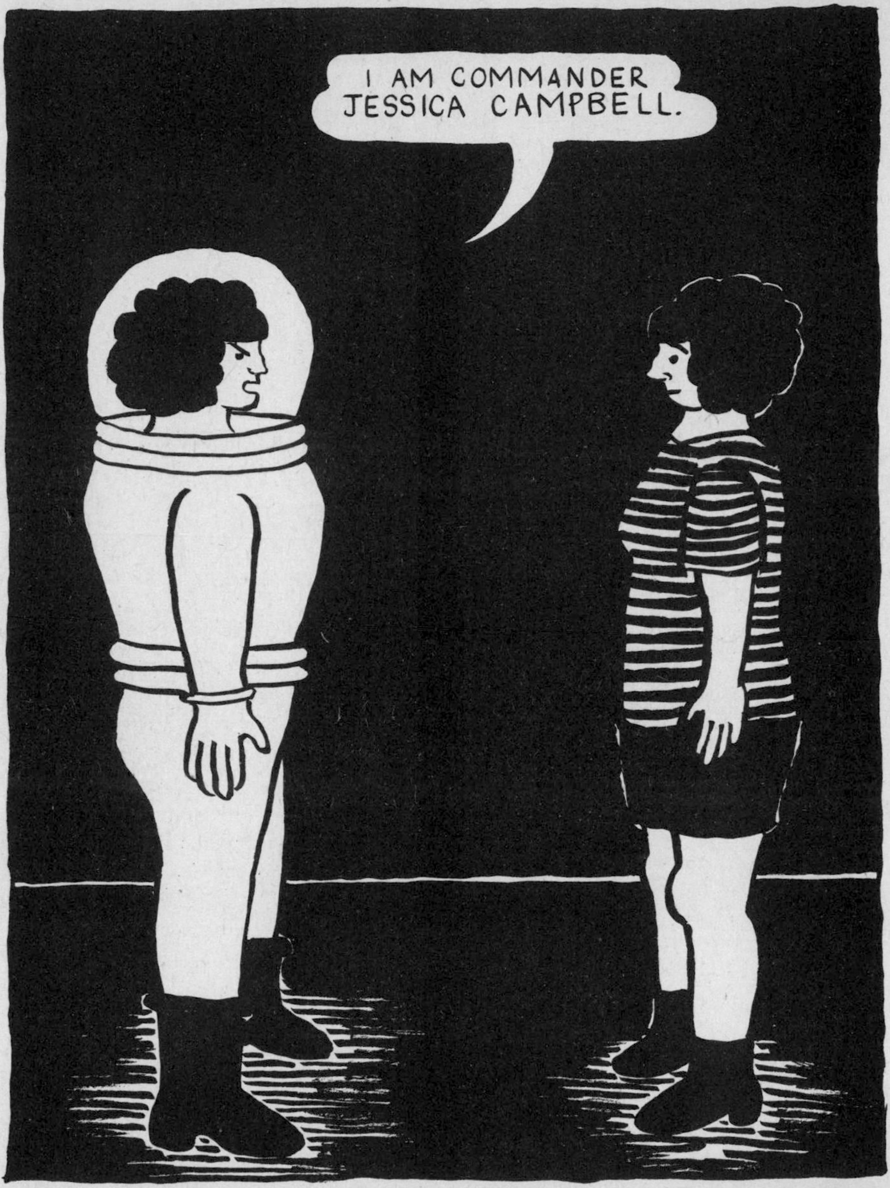
I AM COMMANDER JESSICA CAMPBELL.

CHAPTER 2:
NE OBLIVISCARIS

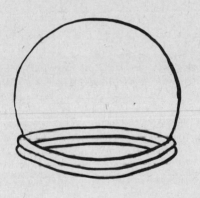

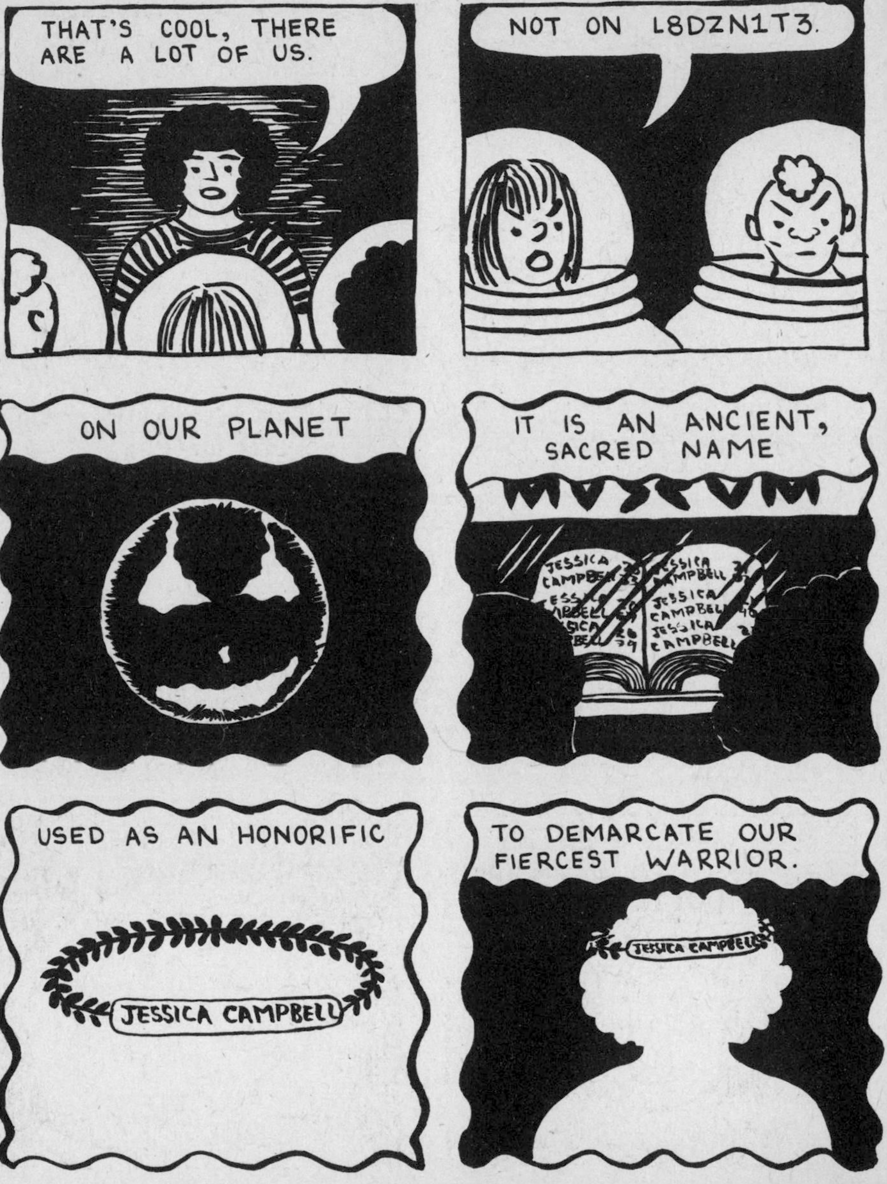
THAT'S COOL, THERE ARE A LOT OF US.
NOT ON L8DZN1T3.
ON OUR PLANET
IT IS AN ANCIENT, SACRED NAME
USED AS AN HONORIFIC
JESSICA CAMPBELL
TO DEMARCATE OUR FIERCEST WARRIOR.
JESSICA CAMPBELL

FOR HUNDREDS OF YEARS, FEMMES HAVE FOUGHT FOR THIS TITLE

AND, AS THERE MAY ONLY BE ONE

THESE FIGHTS INEVITABLY END...

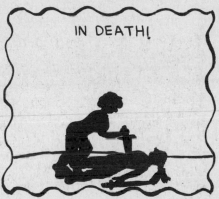

IN DEATH!

HUH, SOUNDS INTENSE.

IT IS INTENSE!

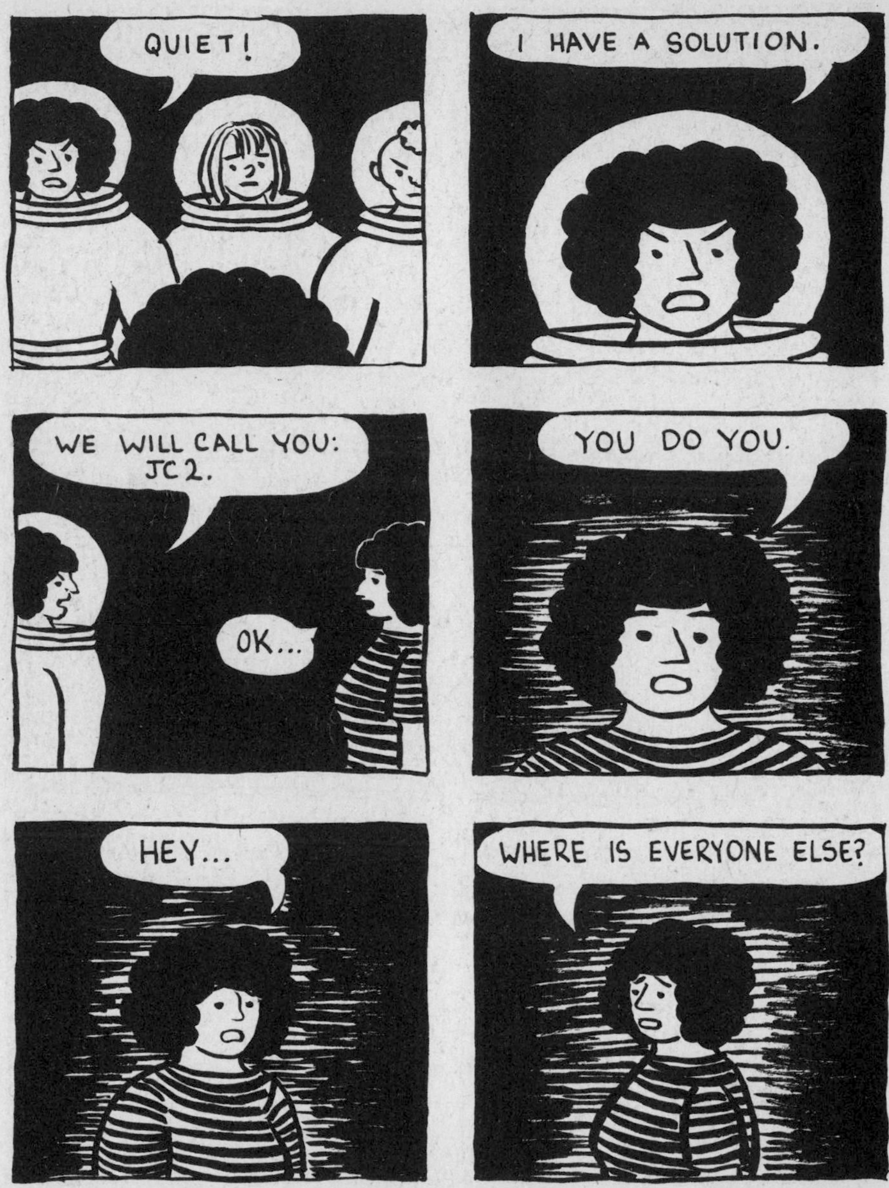
QUIET!
I HAVE A SOLUTION.
WE WILL CALL YOU: JC2.
OK...
YOU DO YOU.
HEY...
WHERE IS EVERYONE ELSE?

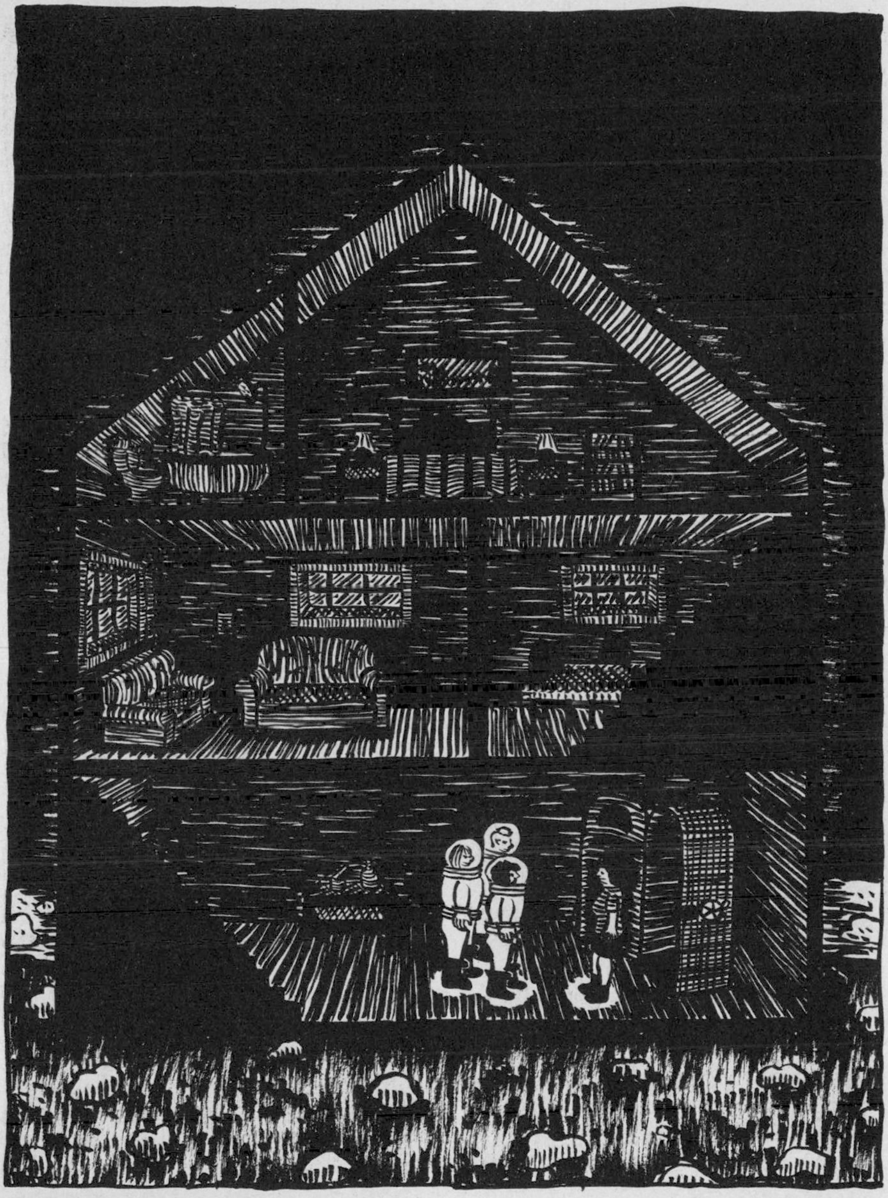

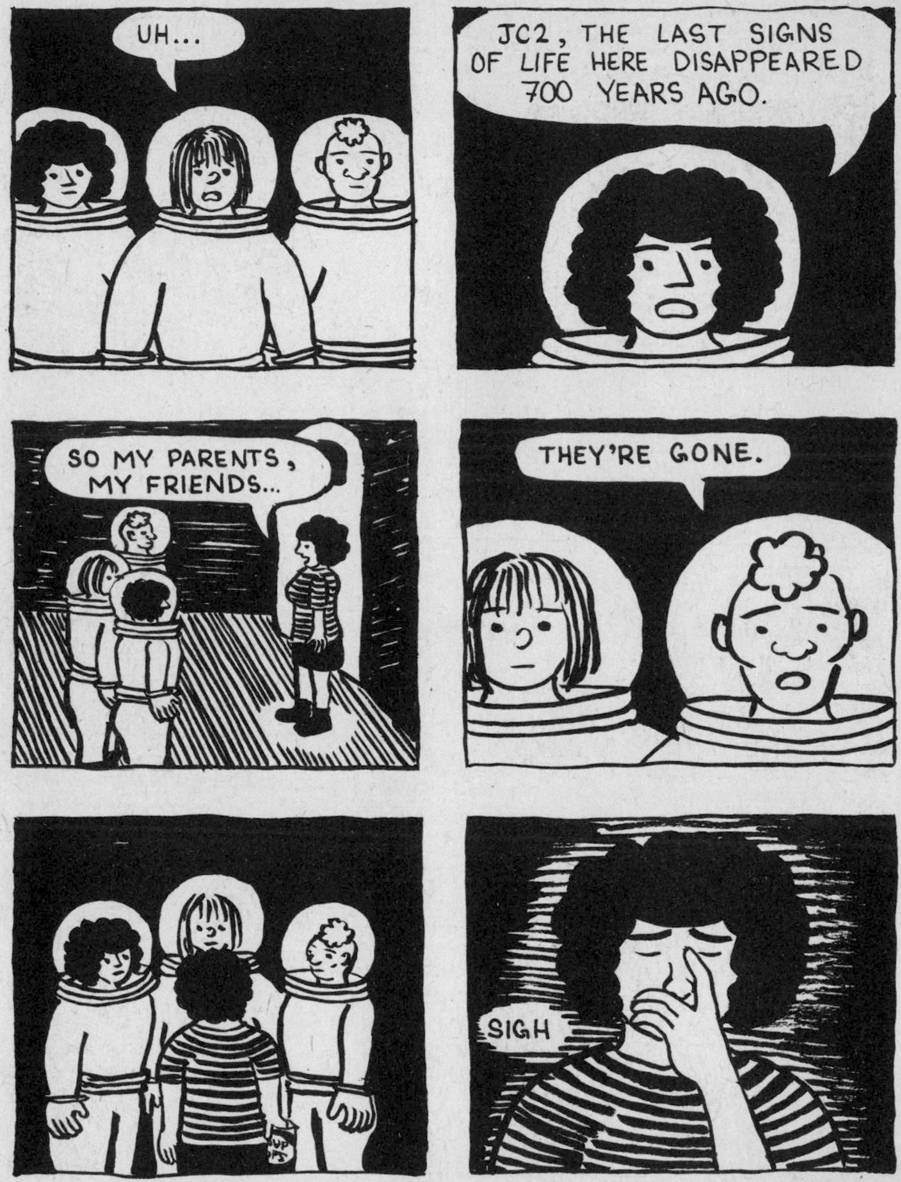
UH...
JC2, THE LAST SIGNS OF LIFE HERE DISAPPEARED 700 YEARS AGO.
SO MY PARENTS, MY FRIENDS...
THEY'RE GONE.
SIGH

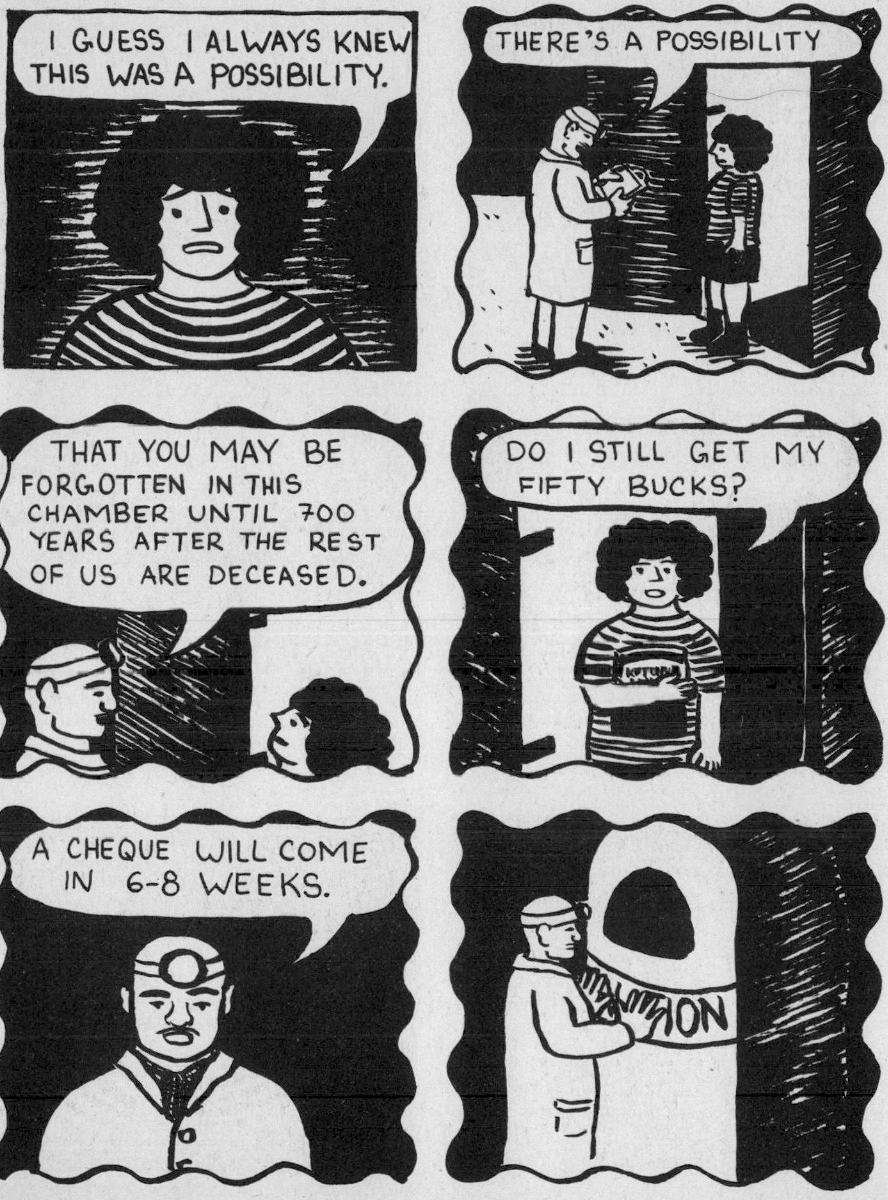
I GUESS I ALWAYS KNEW THIS WAS A POSSIBILITY.
THERE'S A POSSIBILITY
THAT YOU MAY BE FORGOTTEN IN THIS CHAMBER UNTIL 700 YEARS AFTER THE REST OF US ARE DECEASED.
DO I STILL GET MY FIFTY BUCKS?
A CHEQUE WILL COME IN 6-8 WEEKS.

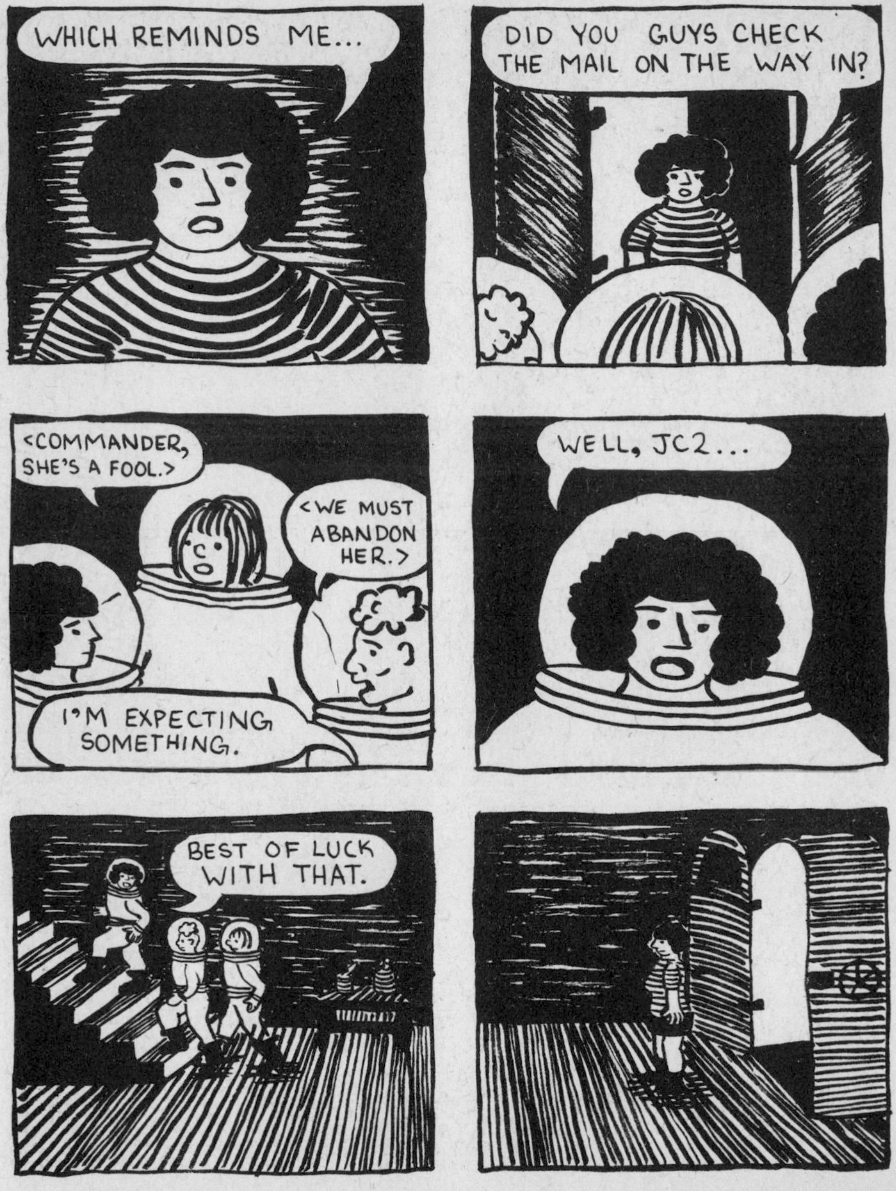
WHICH REMINDS ME...
DID YOU GUYS CHECK THE MAIL ON THE WAY IN?
<COMMANDER, SHE'S A FOOL.>
<WE MUST ABANDON HER.>
I'M EXPECTING SOMETHING.
WELL, JC2...
BEST OF LUCK WITH THAT.

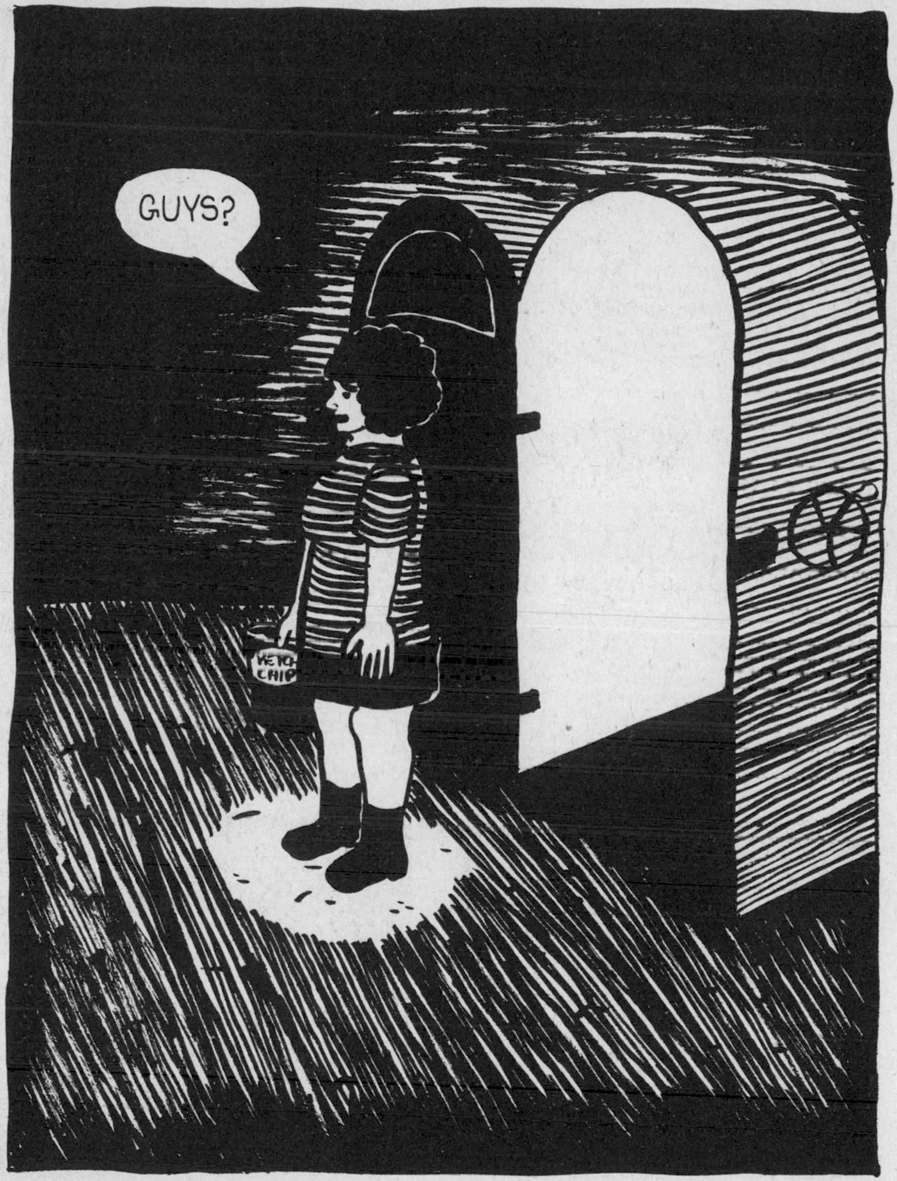
GUYS?

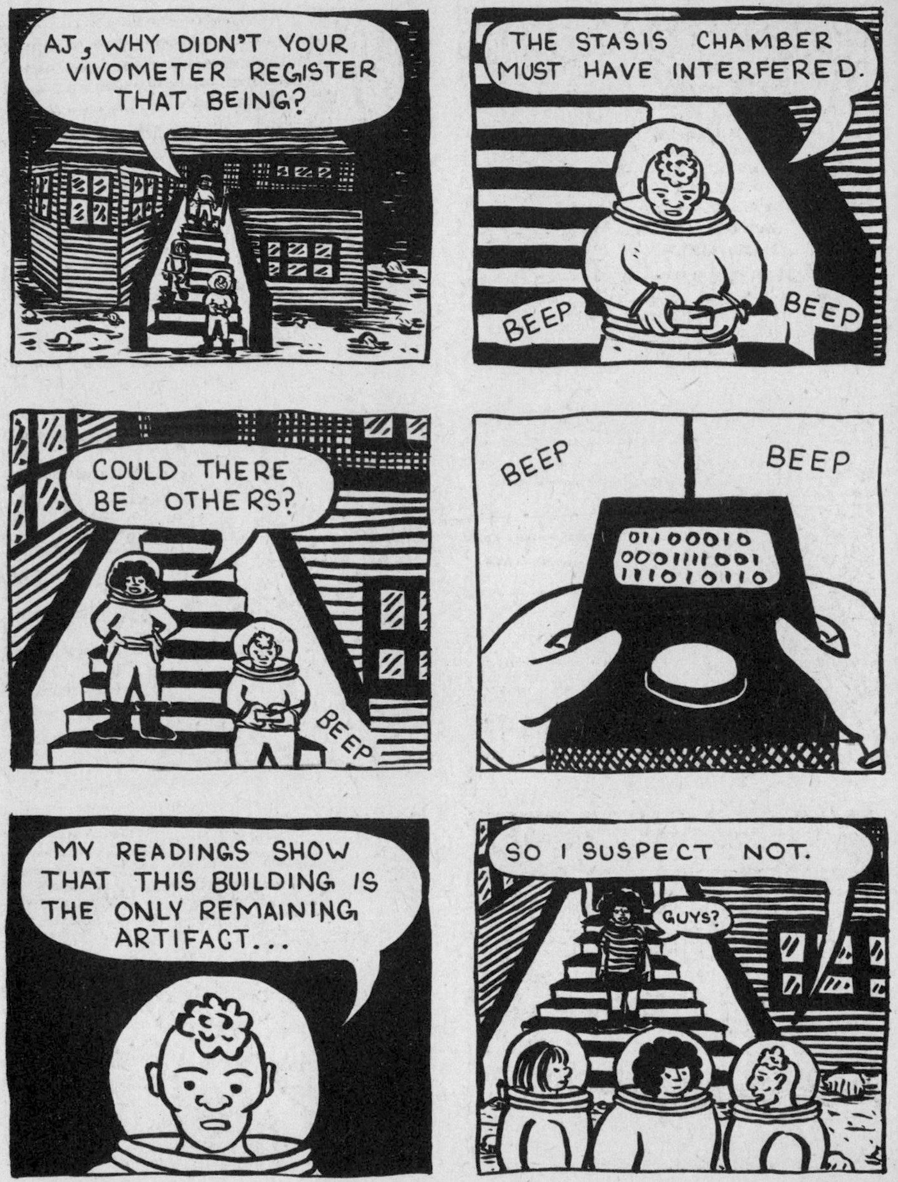
AJ, WHY DIDN'T YOUR VIVOMETER REGISTER THAT BEING?
THE STASIS CHAMBER MUST HAVE INTERFERED.
BEEP
BEEP
COULD THERE BE OTHERS?
BEEP
BEEP
BEEP
011000010
000111001
111010110
MY READINGS SHOW THAT THIS BUILDING IS THE ONLY REMAINING ARTIFACT...
SO I SUSPECT NOT.
GUYS?

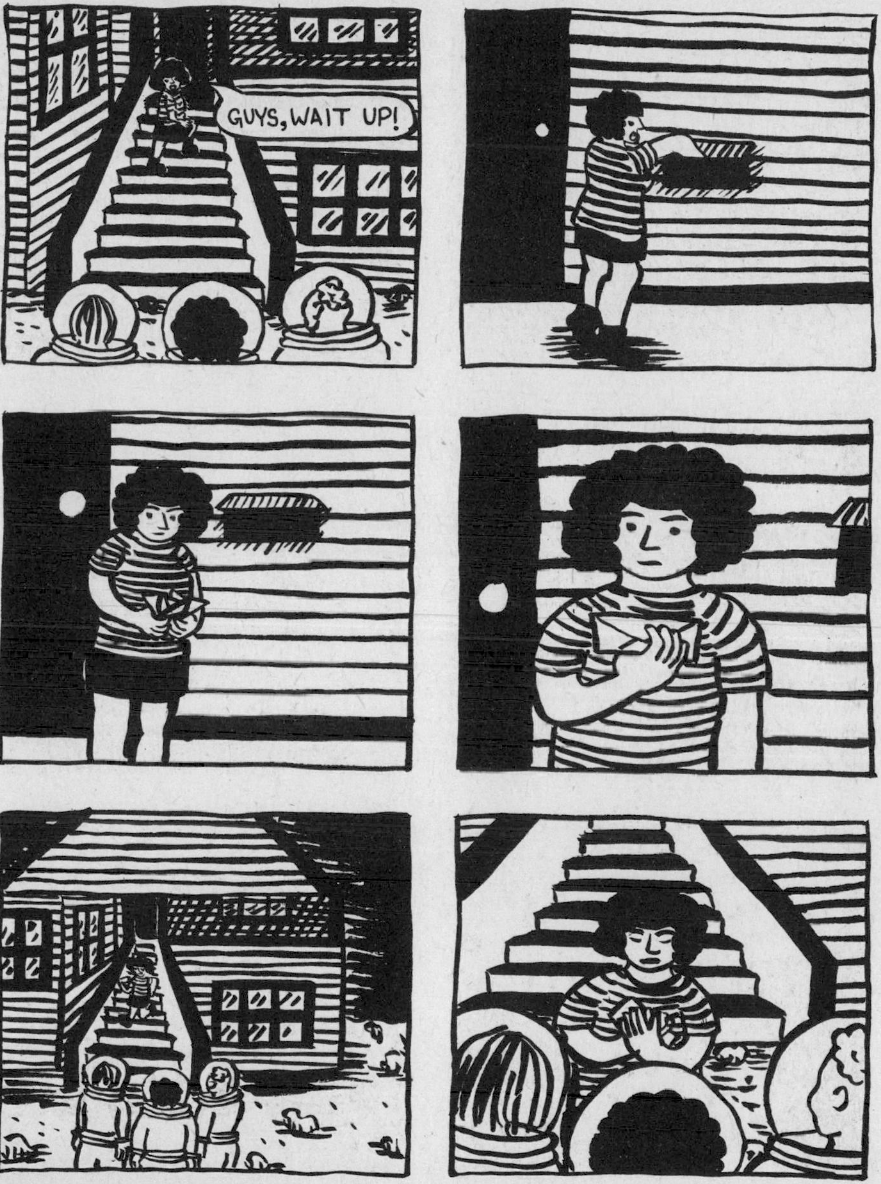
GUYS, WAIT UP!

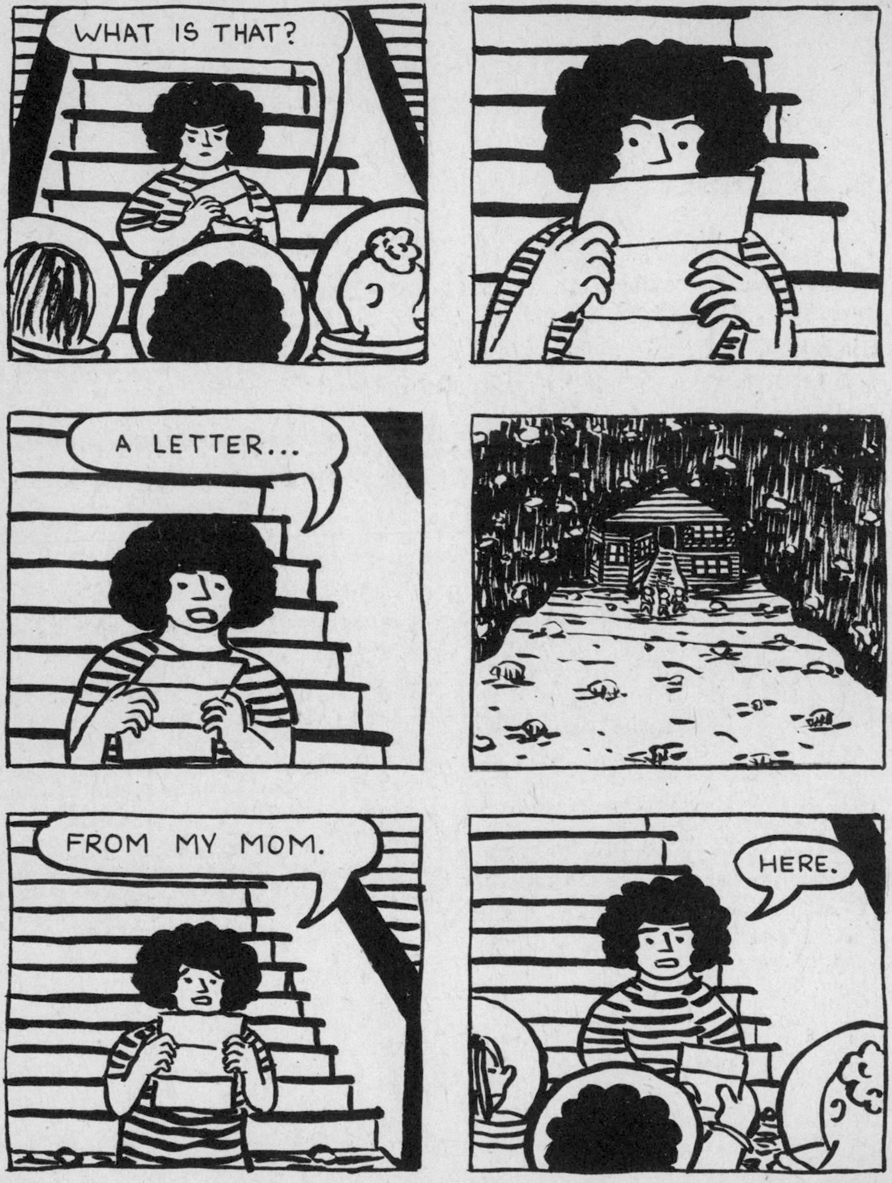
WHAT IS THAT?
A LETTER...
FROM MY MOM.
HERE.

JUNE 21 2020

DEAR JESSICA,

I'M WRITING THIS LETTER UNSURE OF
WHETHER YOU'LL EVER READ IT. TWO
MONTHS AGO, YOU WERE PLACED IN THAT
CHAMBER. TWO WEEKS AGO, NORTH KOREA
LAUNCHED NUCLEAR AND BIOLOGICAL
ATTACKS ON THE U.S. THIS BEGAN
A WORLD WAR THAT HAS, AT THIS
POINT, DESTROYED NEARLY ALL HUMAN
LIFE.

IT APPEARS THE WHOLE PLANET IS
INFECTED WITH RADIATION, SO WE ARE
GOING TO LEAVE YOU IN YOUR CHAMBER,
SUPPOSEDLY AIRTIGHT FOR 1000 YEARS.
IT MAKES ME SAD TO DO THIS, BUT
YOUR POSSIBLE SAFETY IS TOO MUCH
TO RISK.

DAD, AARON, TAYLOR, KYLE AND I HAVE
MADE CONTACT WITH A GROUP IN
AUSTRALIA WHO ARE GOING TO TRY
TO LEAVE THE PLANET. IF WE ARE
SUCCESSFUL, I PRAY WE CAN RETURN
FOR YOU.

I LOVE YOU ALWAYS,
   MOM

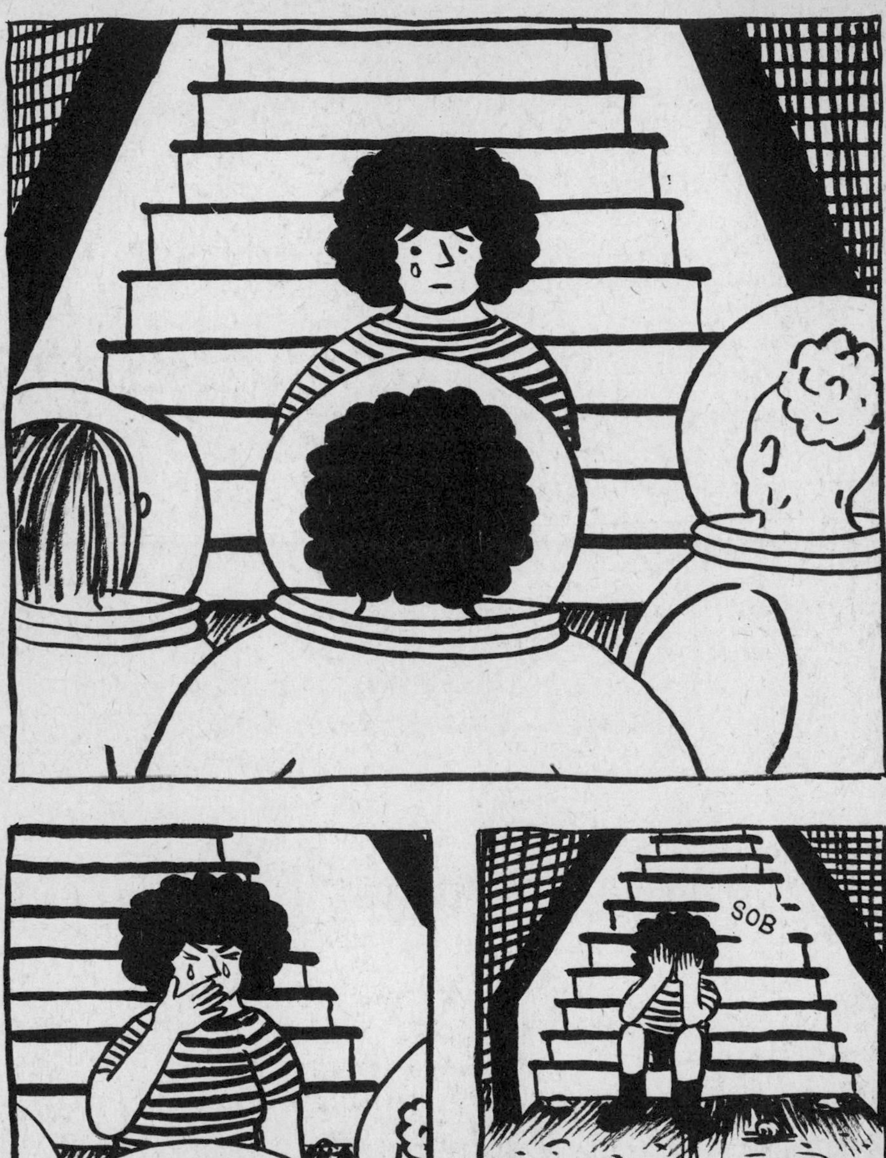
SOB

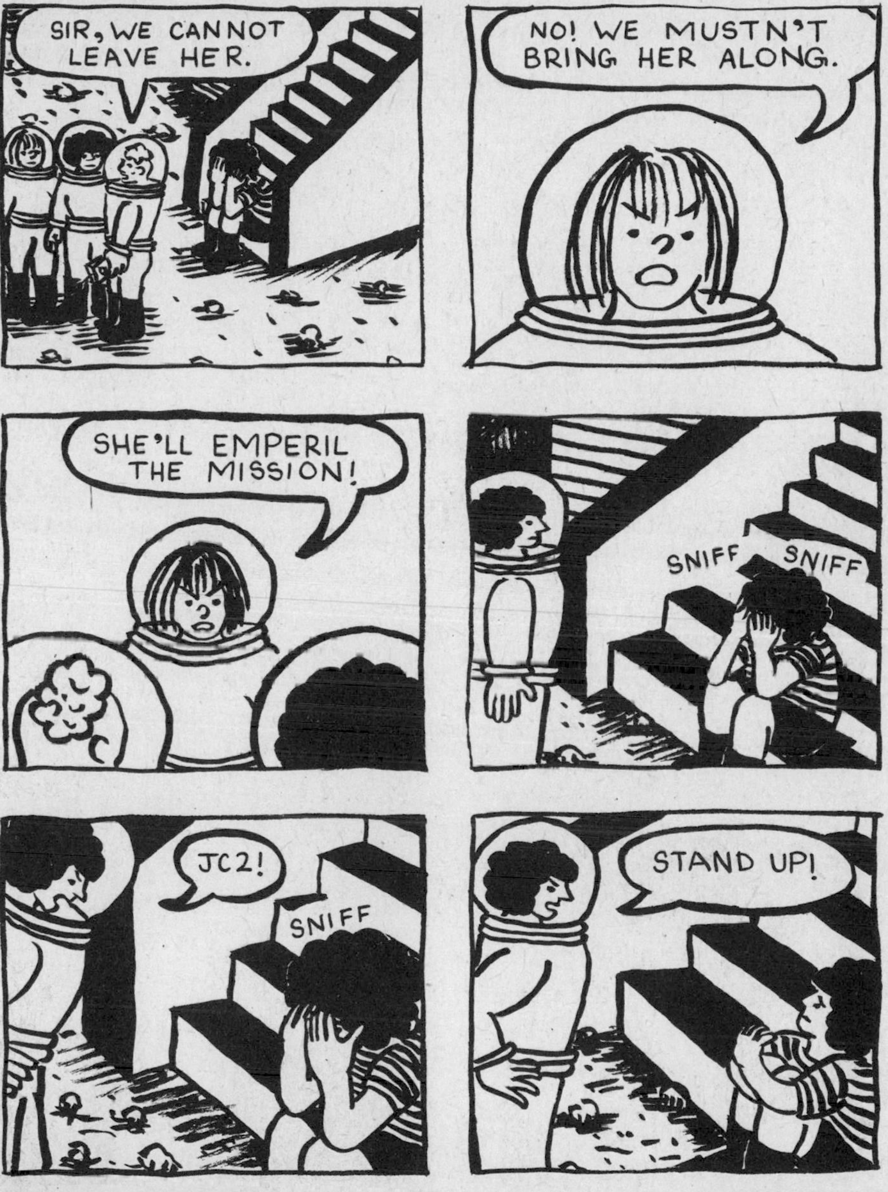
SIR, WE CANNOT LEAVE HER.
NO! WE MUSTN'T BRING HER ALONG.
SHE'LL EMPERIL THE MISSION!
SNIFF
SNIFF
JC2!
SNIFF
STAND UP!

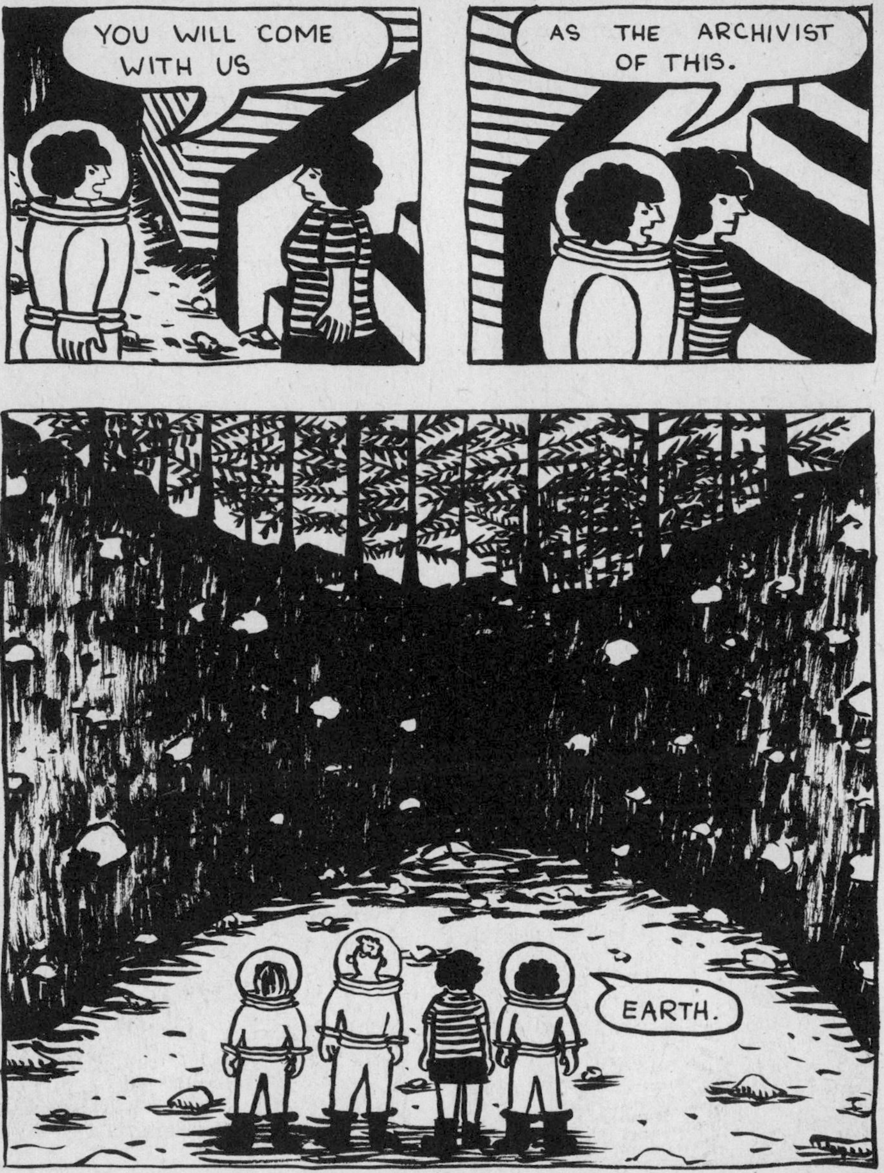
YOU WILL COME WITH US
AS THE ARCHIVIST OF THIS.
EARTH.

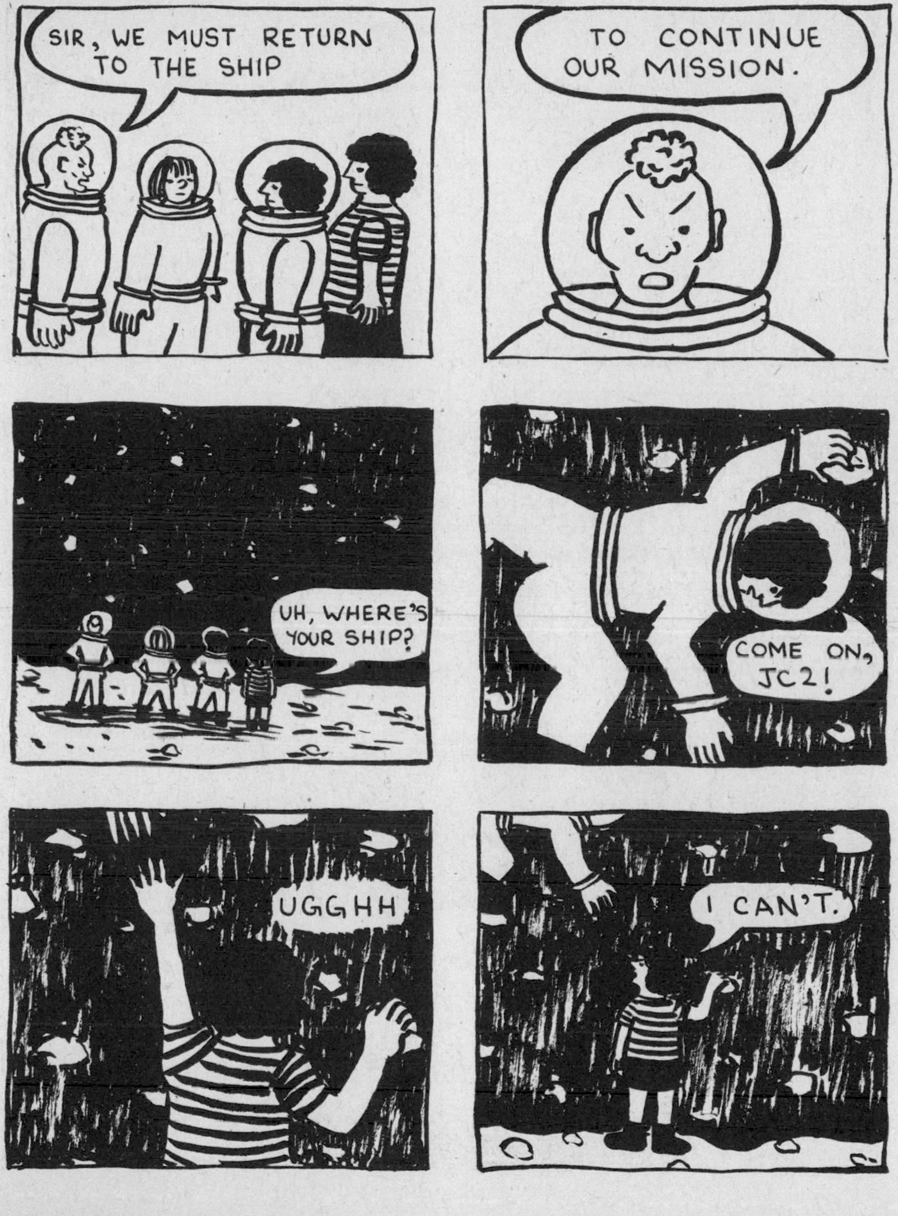
SIR, WE MUST RETURN TO THE SHIP
TO CONTINUE OUR MISSION.
UH, WHERE'S YOUR SHIP?
COME ON, JC2!
UGGHH
I CAN'T.

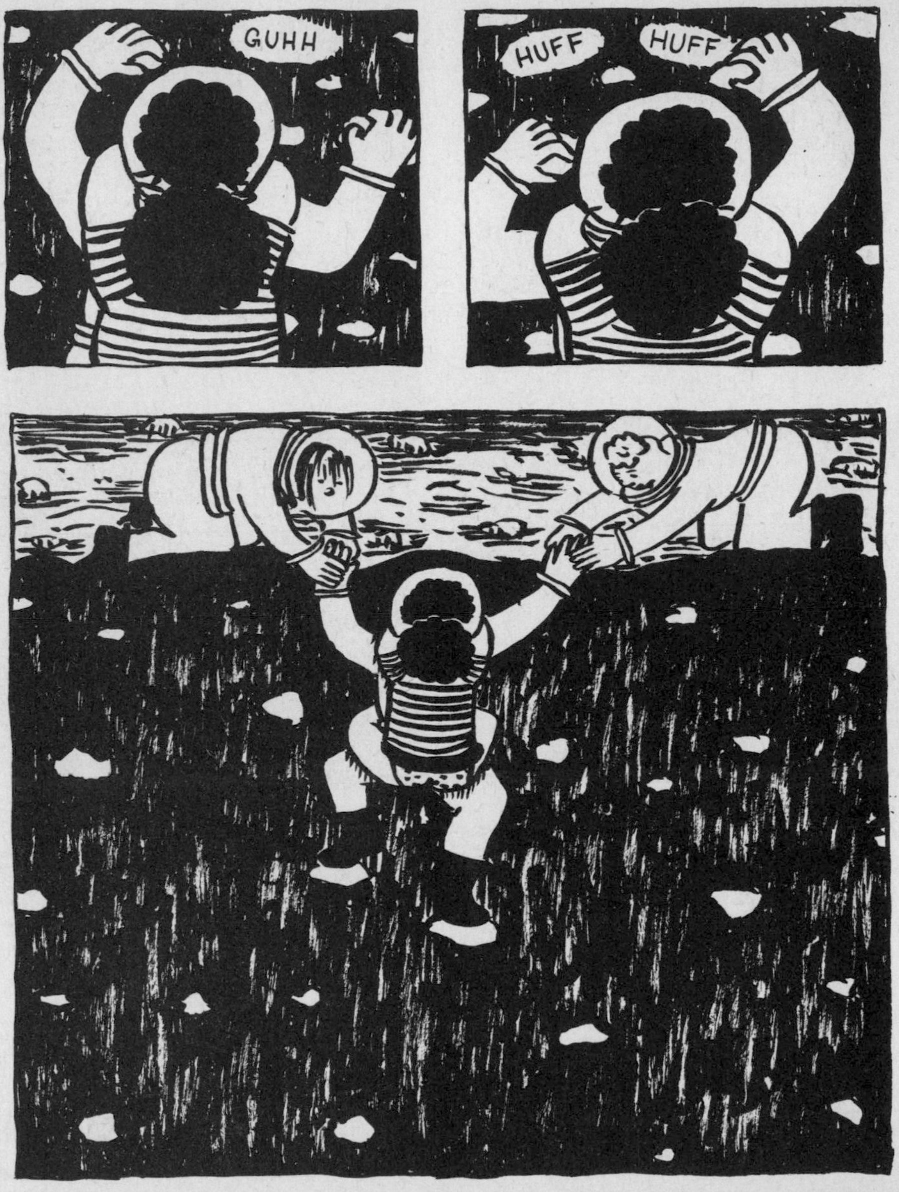
GUHH
HUFF
HUFF

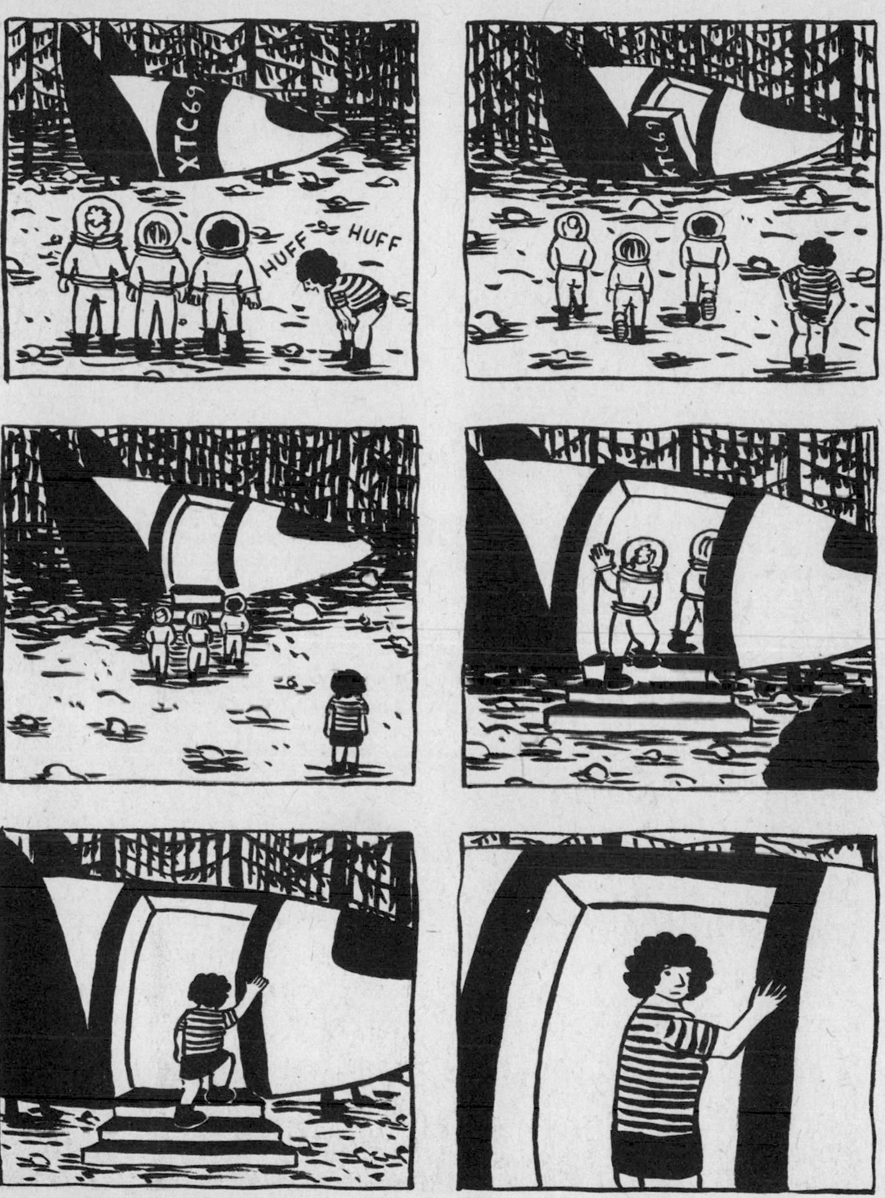
XTC69
HUFF
HUFF
XTC69

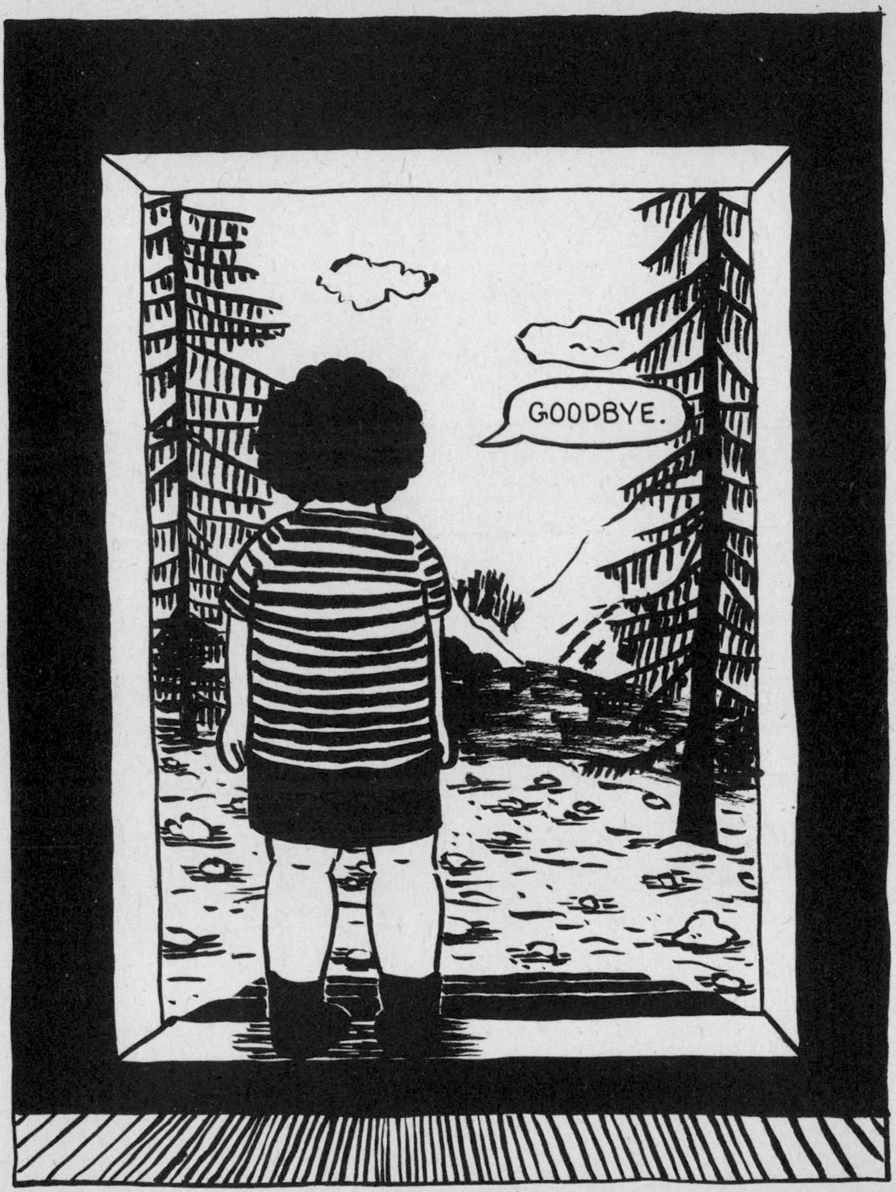
GOODBYE.

CHAPTER 3:
VIGILA LABORA ET ORA

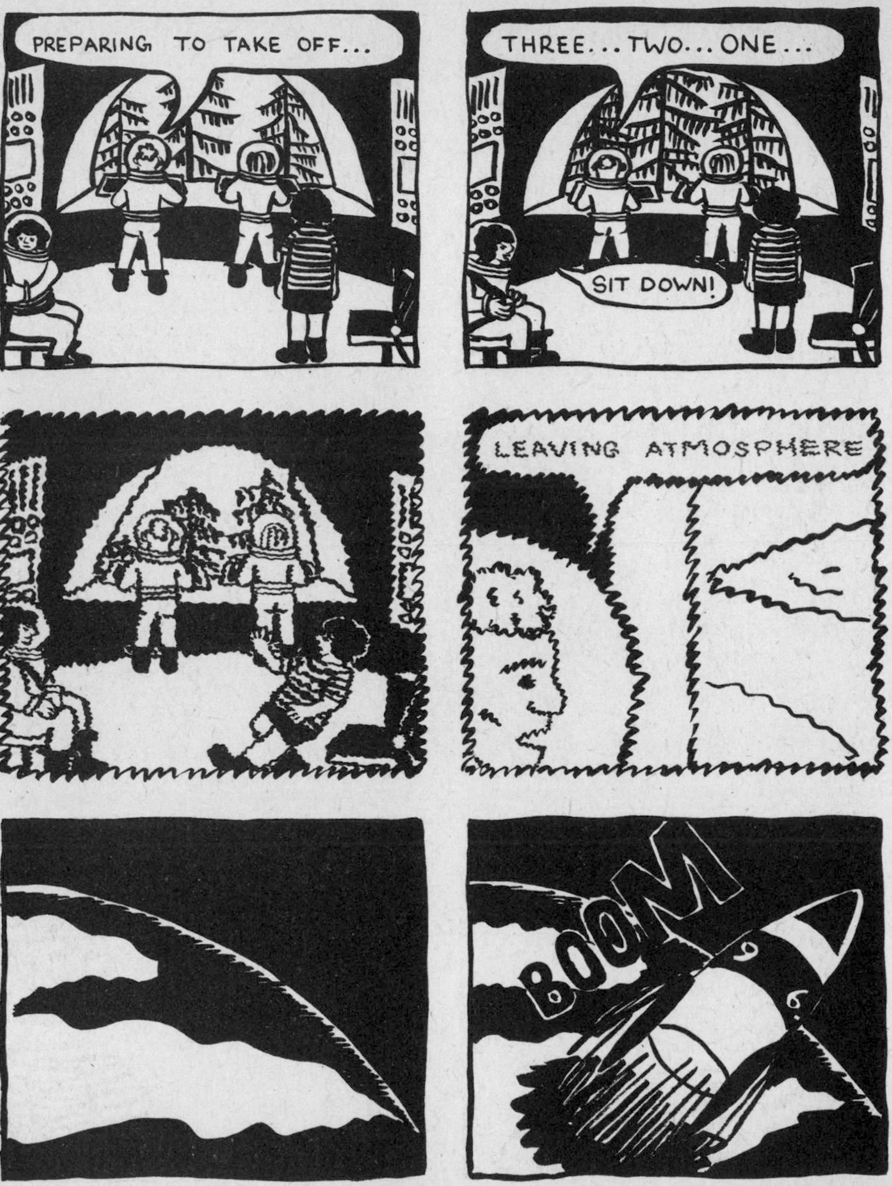
PREPARING TO TAKE OFF...
THREE... TWO... ONE...
SIT DOWN!
LEAVING ATMOSPHERE
BOOM

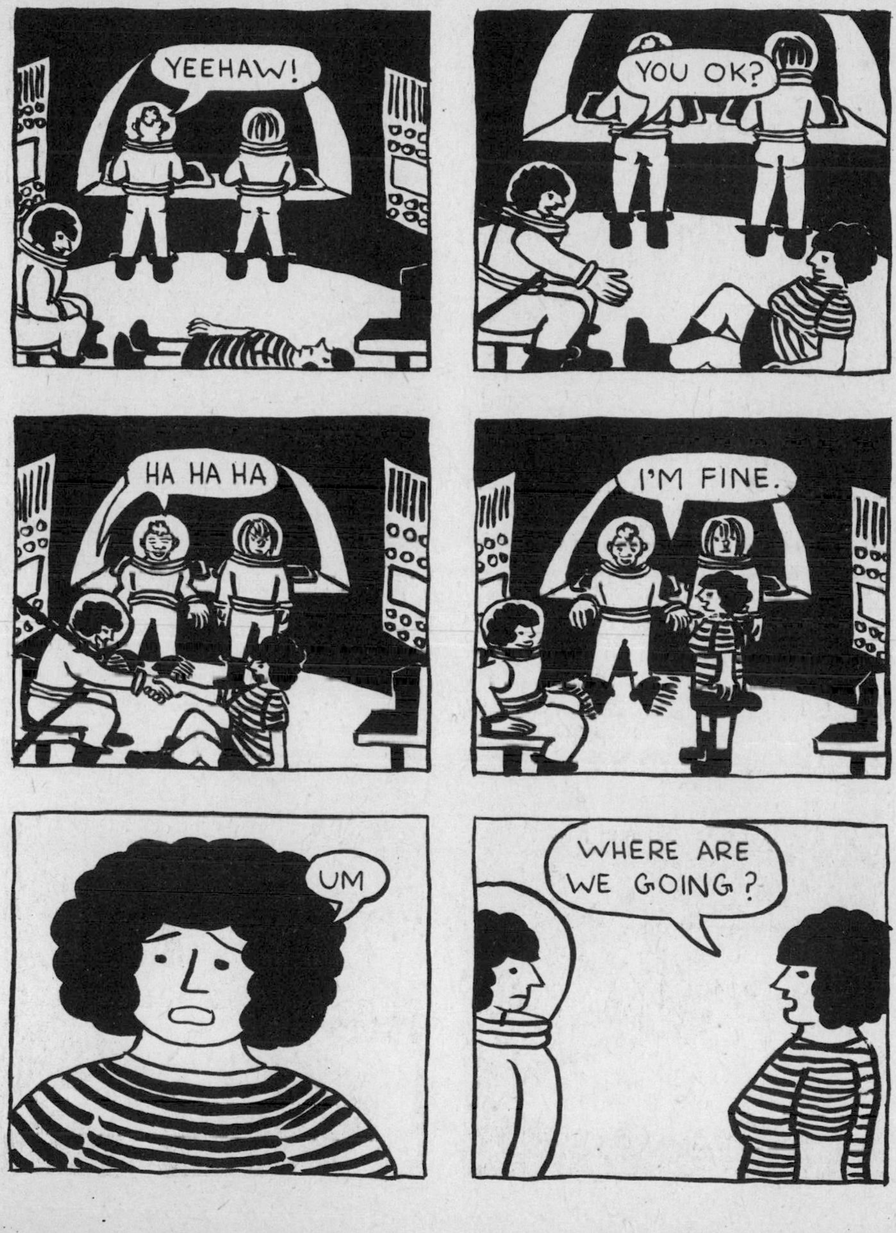
YEEHAW!
YOU OK?
HA HA HA
I'M FINE.
UM
WHERE ARE WE GOING?

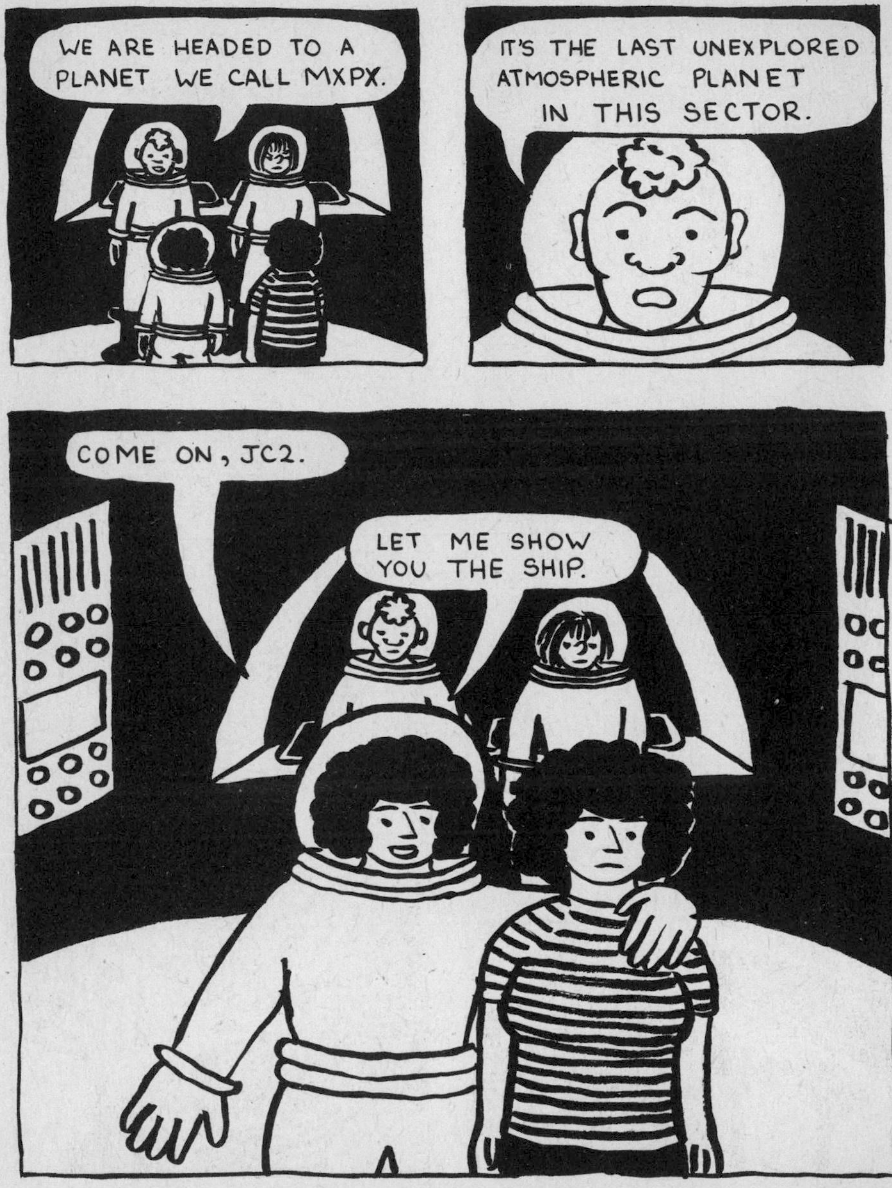
WE ARE HEADED TO A PLANET WE CALL MXPX.
IT'S THE LAST UNEXPLORED ATMOSPHERIC PLANET IN THIS SECTOR.
COME ON, JC2.
LET ME SHOW YOU THE SHIP.

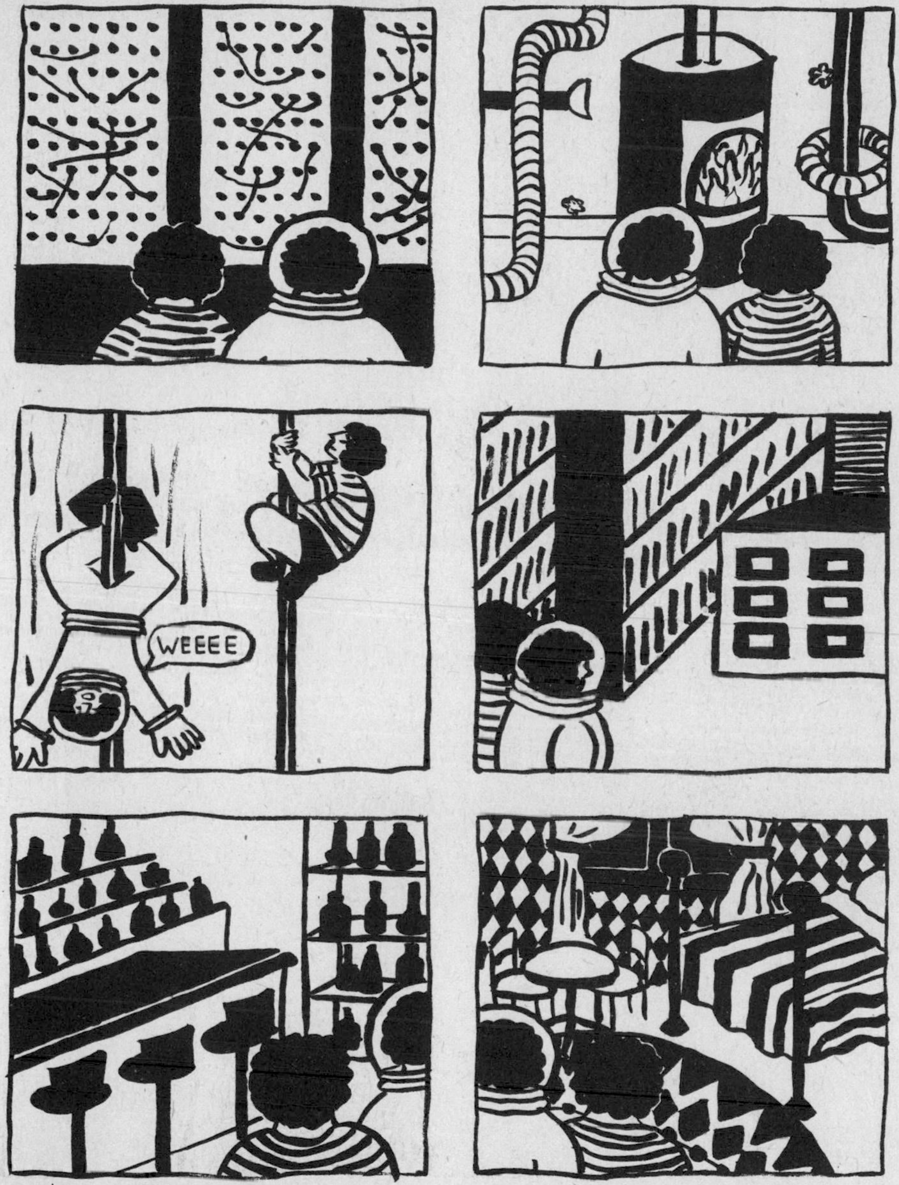
WEEEE

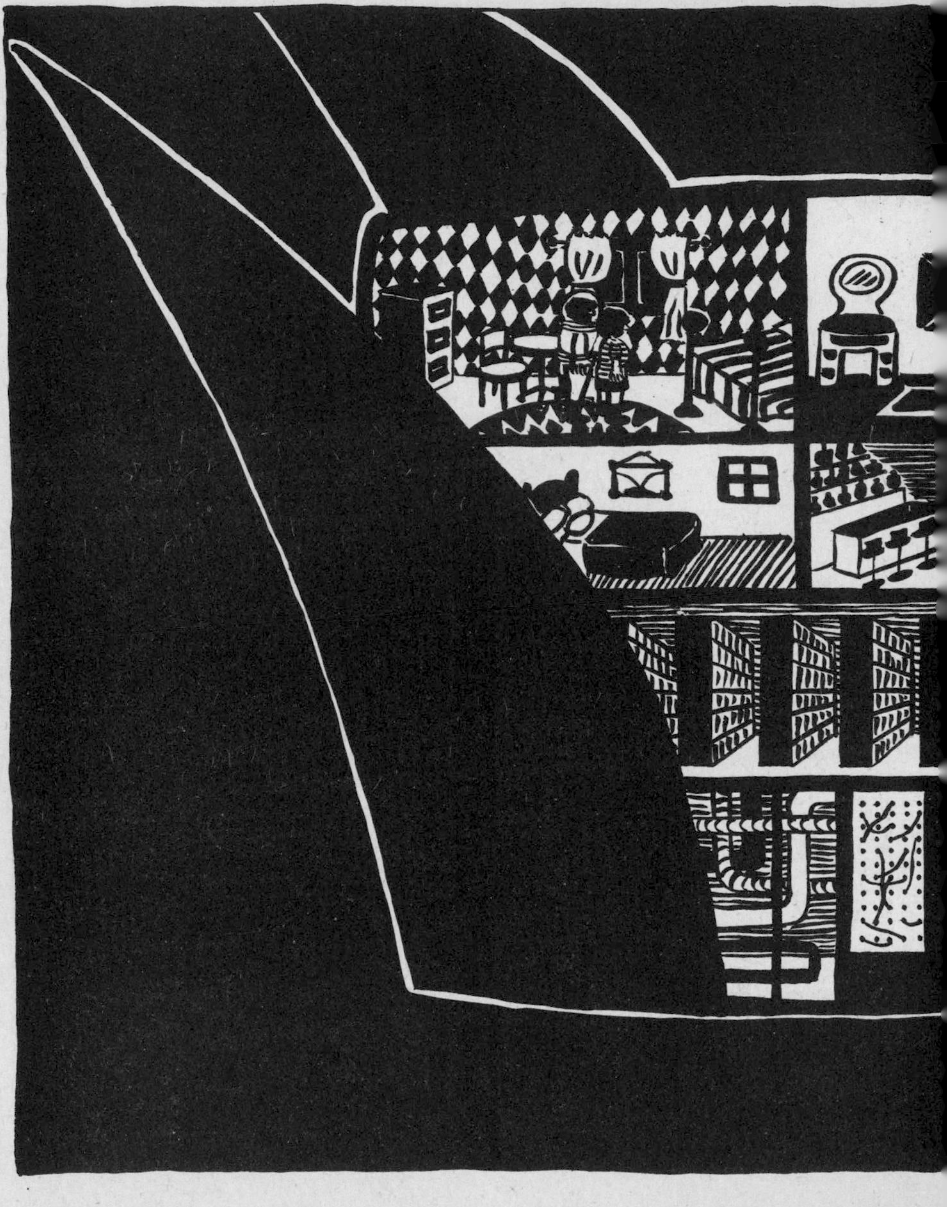

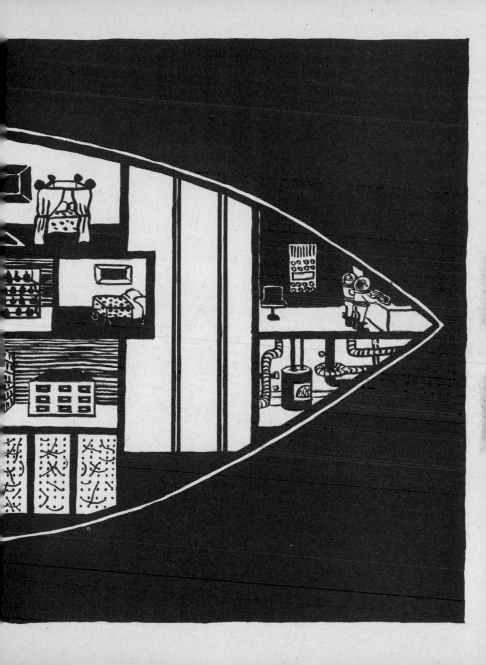

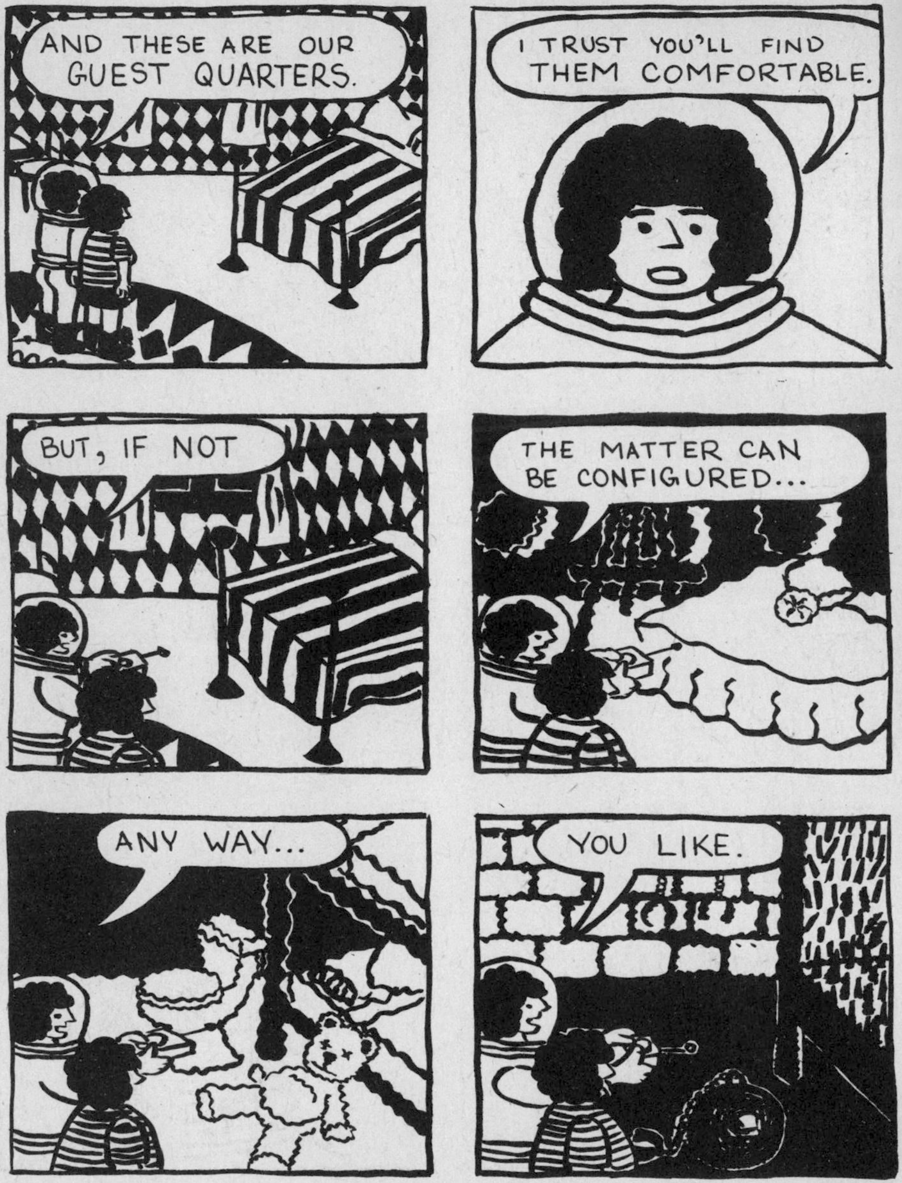
AND THESE ARE OUR GUEST QUARTERS.
I TRUST YOU'LL FIND THEM COMFORTABLE.
BUT, IF NOT
THE MATTER CAN BE CONFIGURED...
ANY WAY...
YOU LIKE.

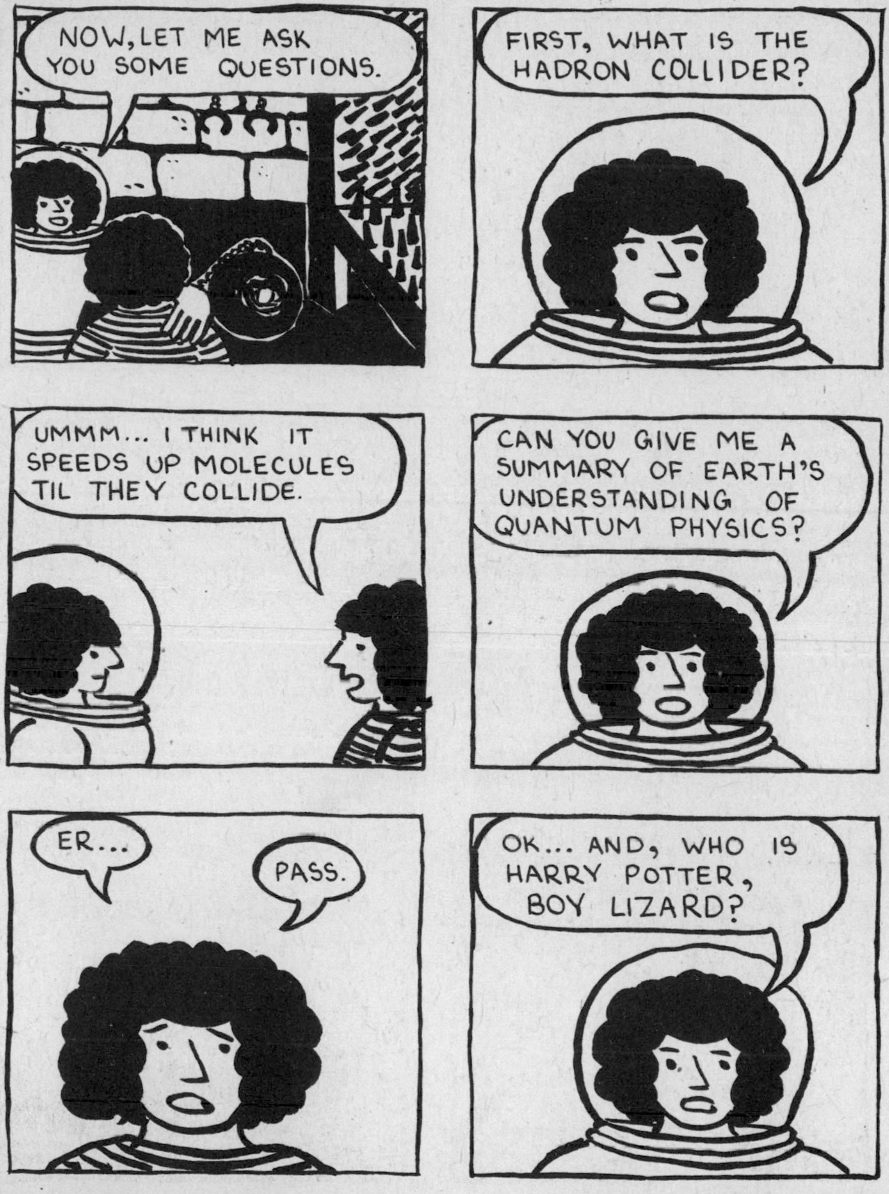
NOW, LET ME ASK YOU SOME QUESTIONS.
FIRST, WHAT IS THE HADRON COLLIDER?
UMMM... I THINK IT SPEEDS UP MOLECULES TIL THEY COLLIDE.
CAN YOU GIVE ME A SUMMARY OF EARTH'S UNDERSTANDING OF QUANTUM PHYSICS?
ER...
PASS.
OK... AND, WHO IS HARRY POTTER, BOY LIZARD?

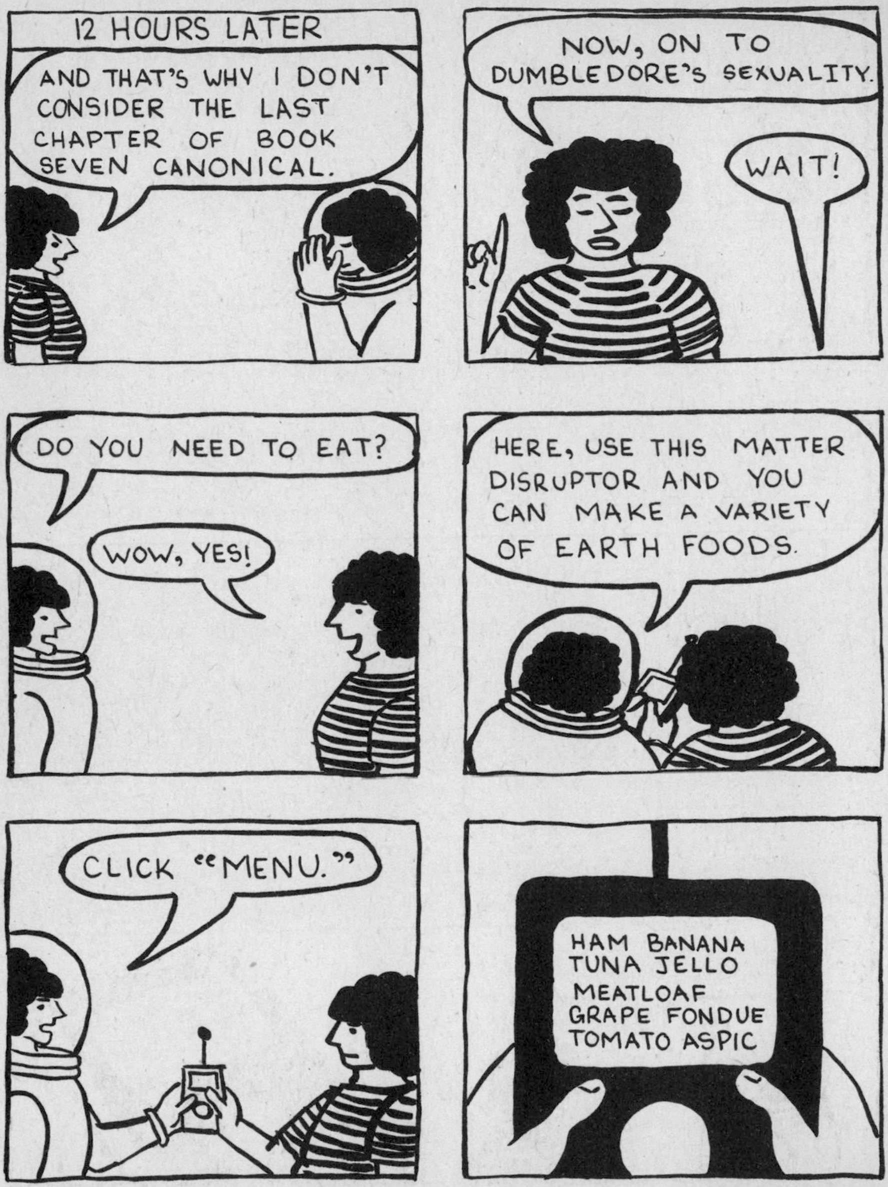
12 HOURS LATER
AND THAT'S WHY I DON'T CONSIDER THE LAST CHAPTER OF BOOK SEVEN CANONICAL.
NOW, ON TO DUMBLEDORE'S SEXUALITY.
WAIT!
DO YOU NEED TO EAT?
WOW, YES!
HERE, USE THIS MATTER DISRUPTOR AND YOU CAN MAKE A VARIETY OF EARTH FOODS.
CLICK "MENU."
HAM BANANA
TUNA JELLO
MEATLOAF
GRAPE FONDUE
TOMATO ASPIC

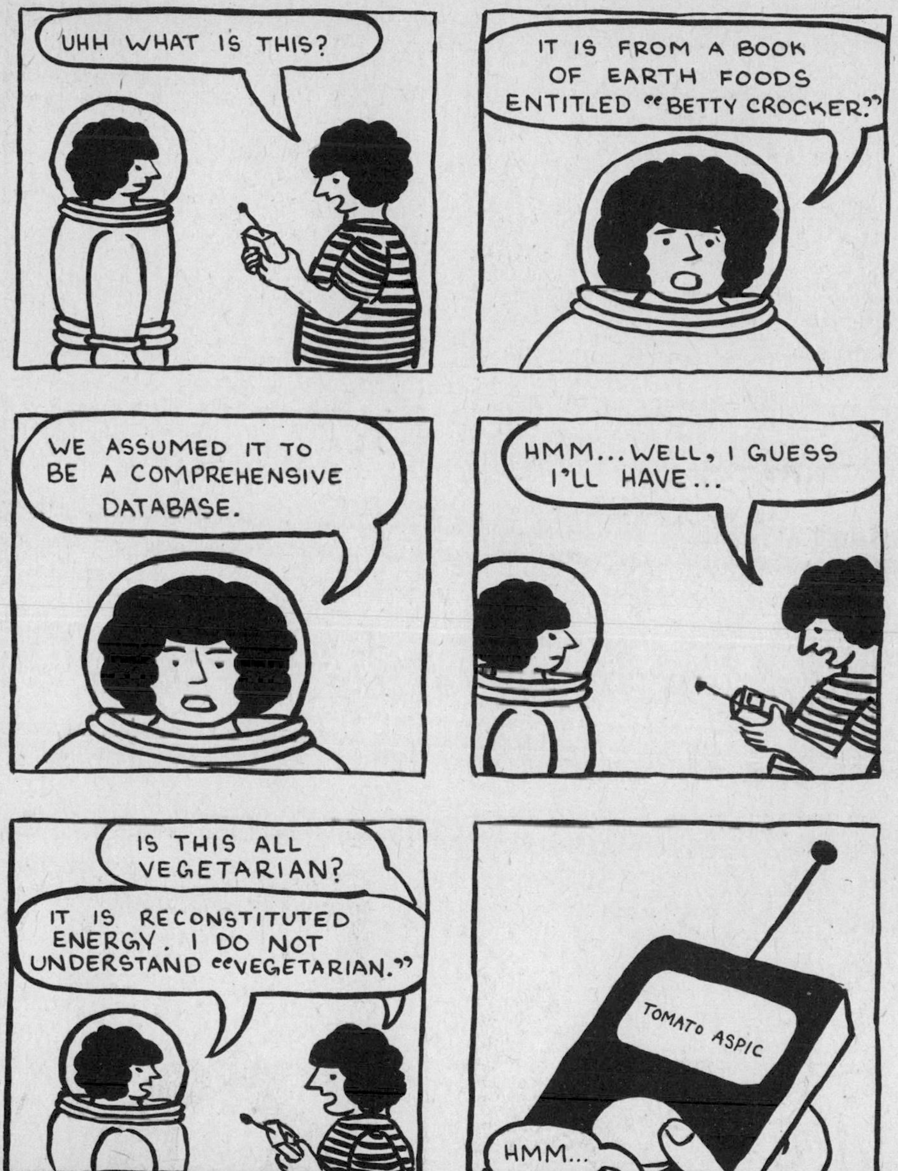
UHH WHAT IS THIS?
IT IS FROM A BOOK OF EARTH FOODS ENTITLED "BETTY CROCKER."
WE ASSUMED IT TO BE A COMPREHENSIVE DATABASE.
HMM... WELL, I GUESS I'LL HAVE...
IS THIS ALL VEGETARIAN?
IT IS RECONSTITUTED ENERGY. I DO NOT UNDERSTAND "VEGETARIAN."
TOMATO ASPIC
HMM...

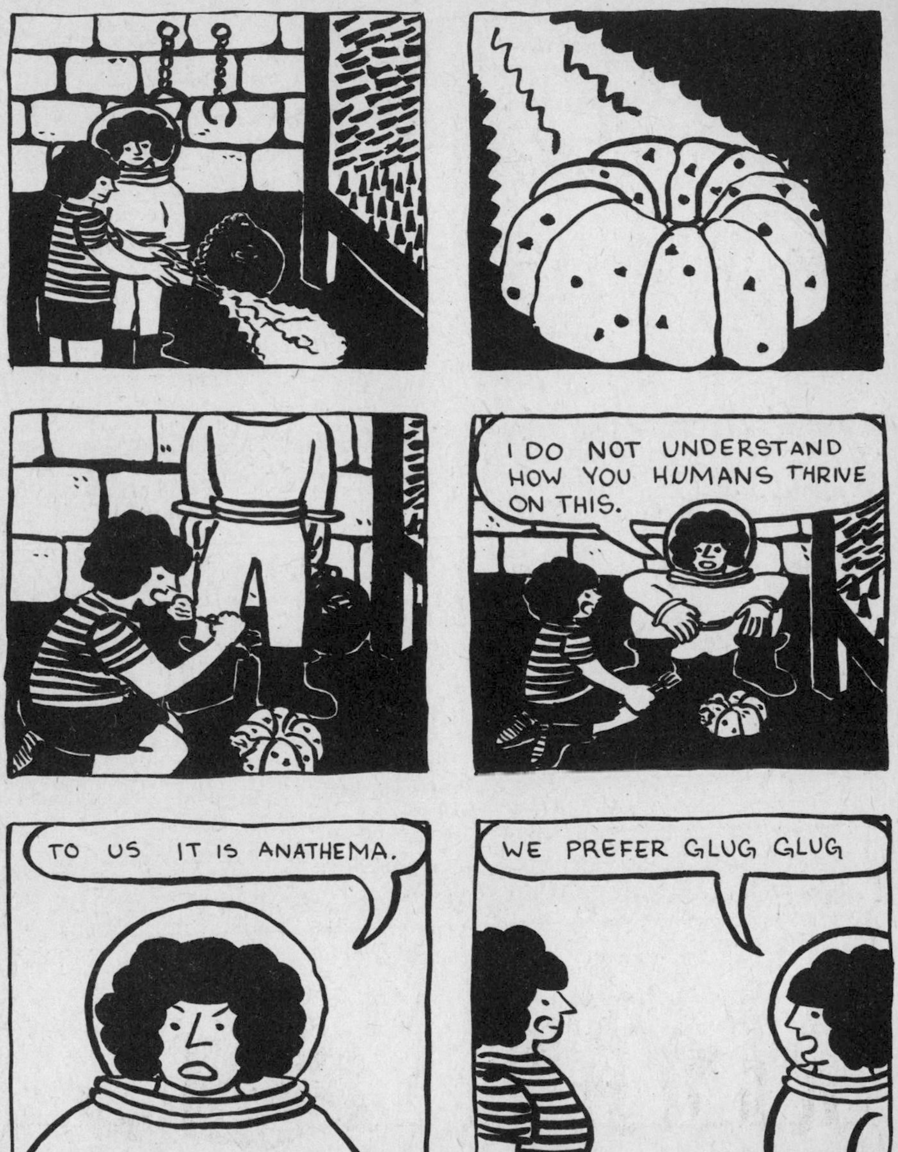
I DO NOT UNDERSTAND HOW YOU HUMANS THRIVE ON THIS.
TO US IT IS ANATHEMA.
WE PREFER GLUG GLUG

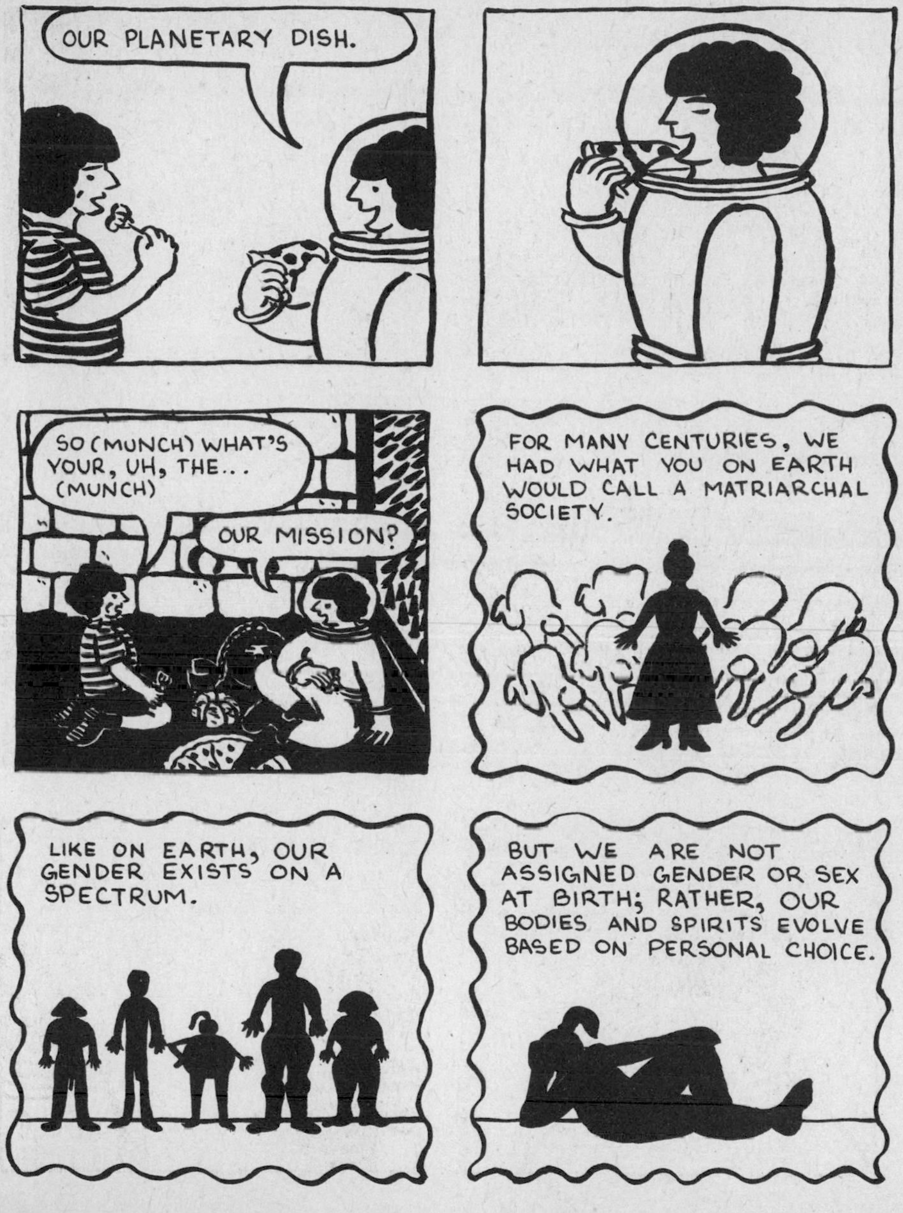
OUR PLANETARY DISH.
SO (MUNCH) WHAT'S YOUR, UH, THE... (MUNCH)
OUR MISSION?
FOR MANY CENTURIES, WE HAD WHAT YOU ON EARTH WOULD CALL A MATRIARCHAL SOCIETY.
LIKE ON EARTH, OUR GENDER EXISTS ON A SPECTRUM.
BUT WE ARE NOT ASSIGNED GENDER OR SEX AT BIRTH; RATHER, OUR BODIES AND SPIRITS EVOLVE BASED ON PERSONAL CHOICE.

AND, AS IT WAS IN EVERY WAY BETTER TO BE "FEMALE"

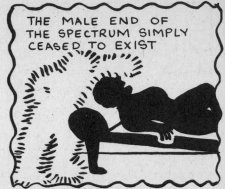

THE MALE END OF THE SPECTRUM SIMPLY CEASED TO EXIST

APPROXIMATELY 300 YEARS AGO.

OUR SOCIETY NOW REPRODUCES EXCLUSIVELY THROUGH CLONING.

WHICH WAS ACCEPTABLE UNTIL RECENTLY

WHEN A PLAGUE ELIMINATED MUCH OF THE POPULATION.

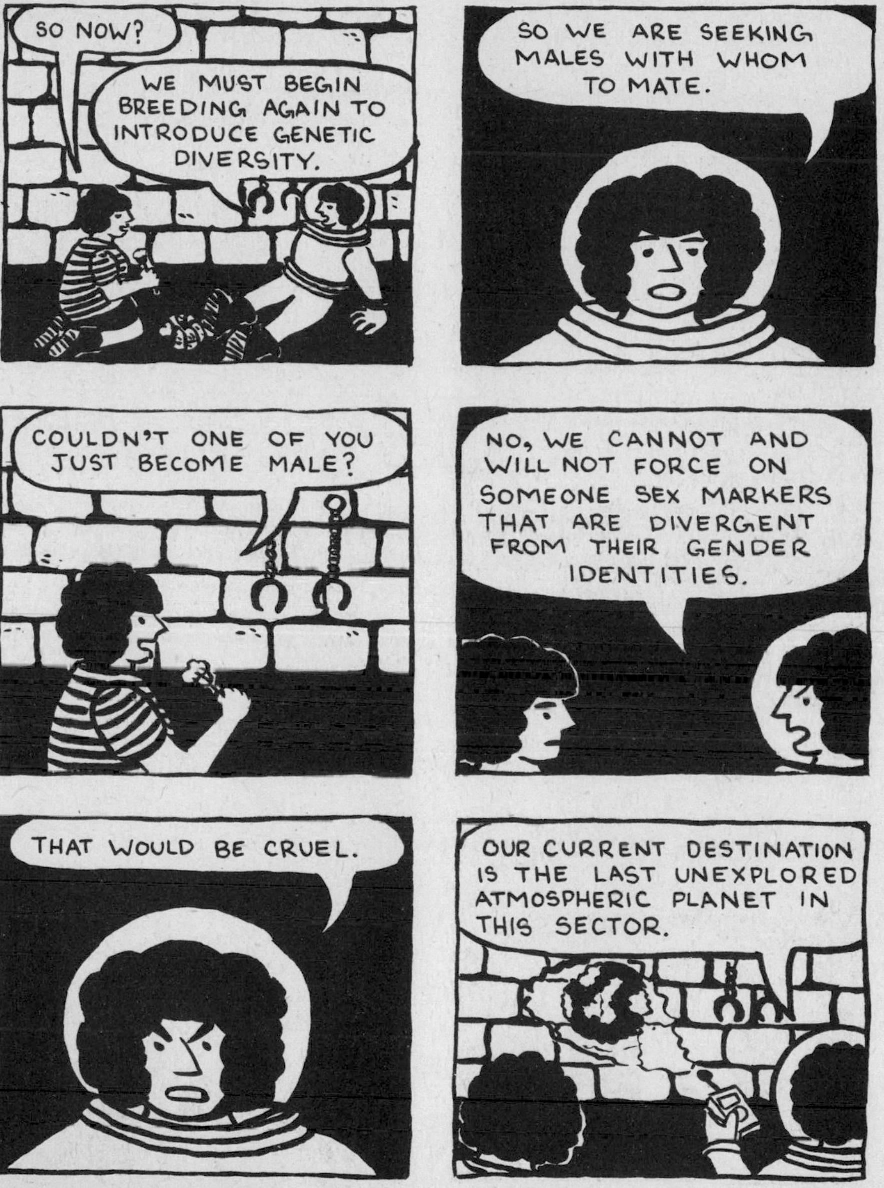
SO NOW?
WE MUST BEGIN BREEDING AGAIN TO INTRODUCE GENETIC DIVERSITY.
SO WE ARE SEEKING MALES WITH WHOM TO MATE.
COULDN'T ONE OF YOU JUST BECOME MALE?
NO, WE CANNOT AND WILL NOT FORCE ON SOMEONE SEX MARKERS THAT ARE DIVERGENT FROM THEIR GENDER IDENTITIES.
THAT WOULD BE CRUEL.
OUR CURRENT DESTINATION IS THE LAST UNEXPLORED ATMOSPHERIC PLANET IN THIS SECTOR.

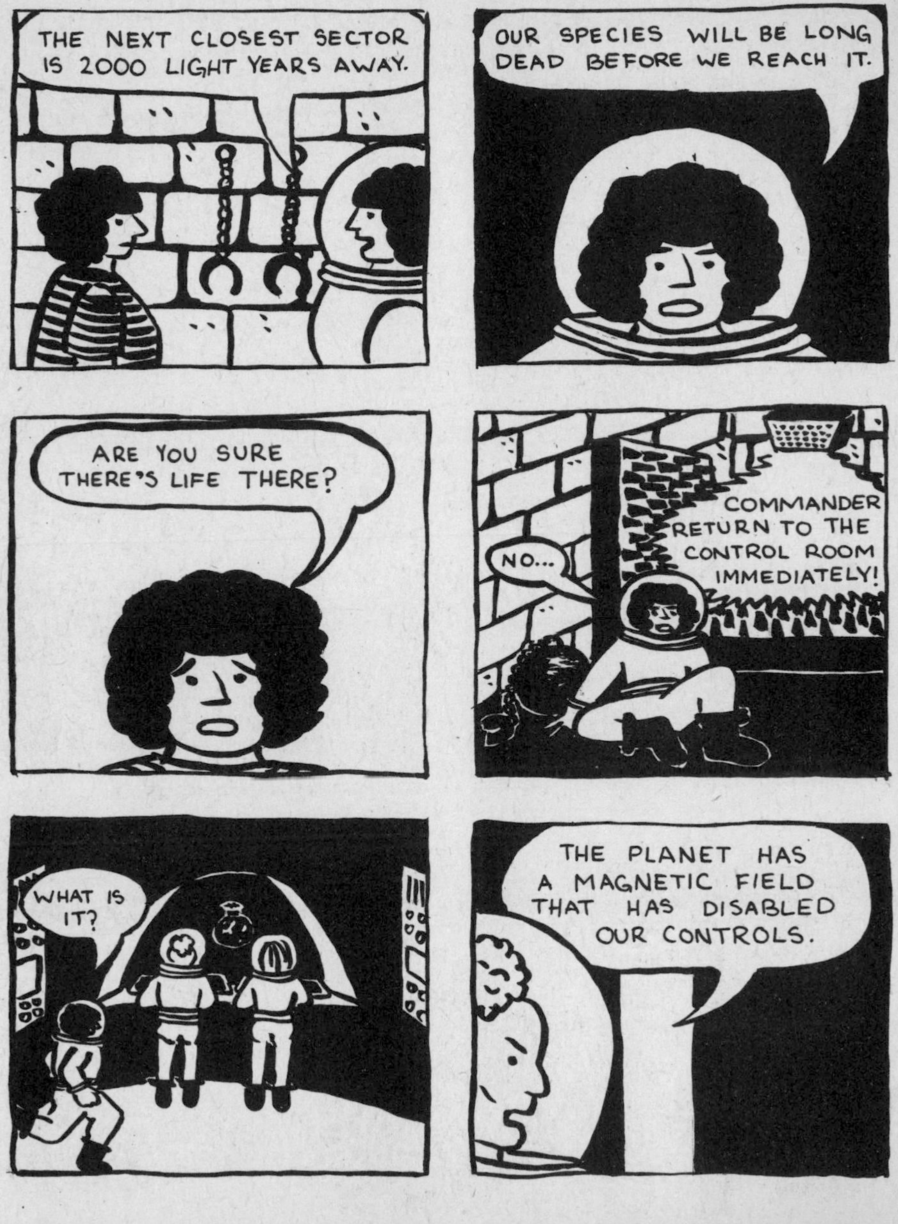
THE NEXT CLOSEST SECTOR IS 2000 LIGHT YEARS AWAY.
OUR SPECIES WILL BE LONG DEAD BEFORE WE REACH IT.
ARE YOU SURE THERE'S LIFE THERE?
COMMANDER RETURN TO THE CONTROL ROOM IMMEDIATELY!
NO...
WHAT IS IT?
THE PLANET HAS A MAGNETIC FIELD THAT HAS DISABLED OUR CONTROLS.

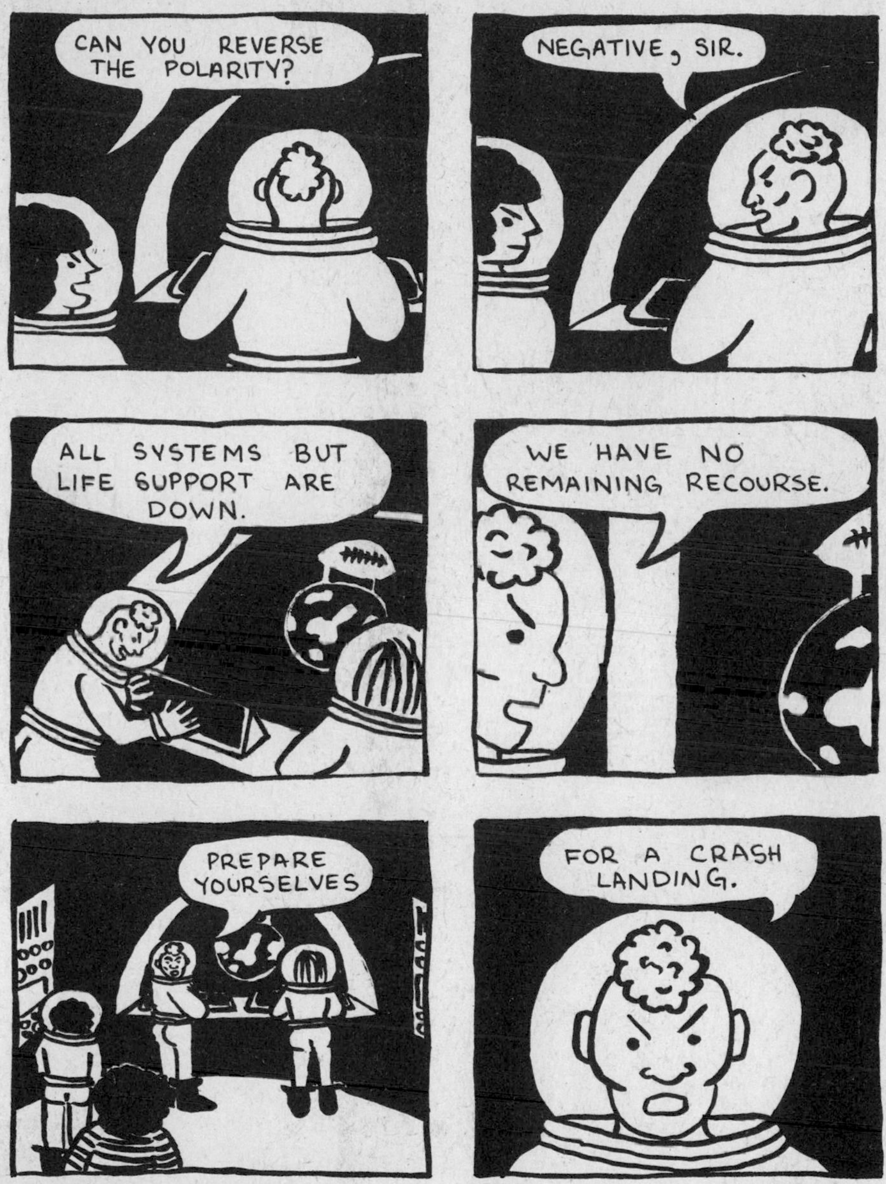
CAN YOU REVERSE THE POLARITY?
NEGATIVE, SIR.
ALL SYSTEMS BUT LIFE SUPPORT ARE DOWN.
WE HAVE NO REMAINING RECOURSE.
PREPARE YOURSELVES
FOR A CRASH LANDING.

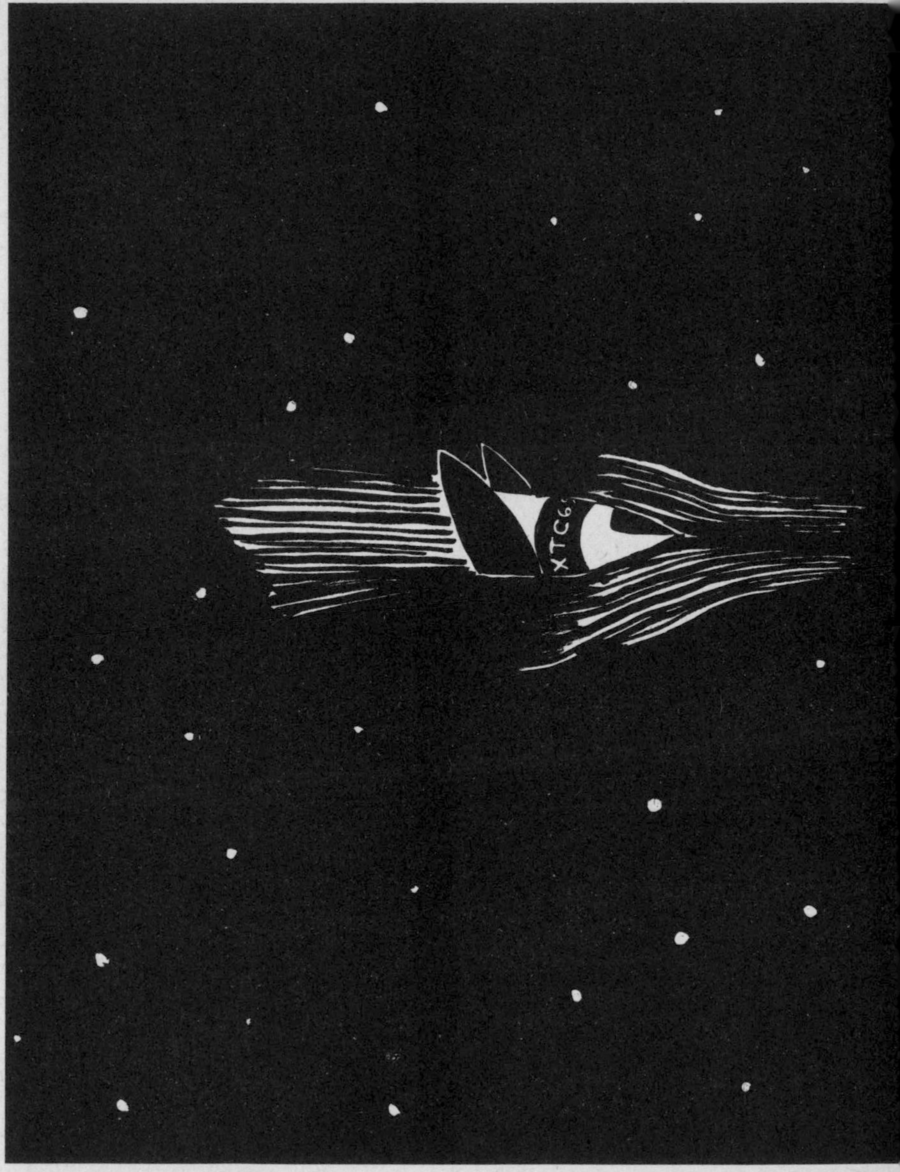
XTC6

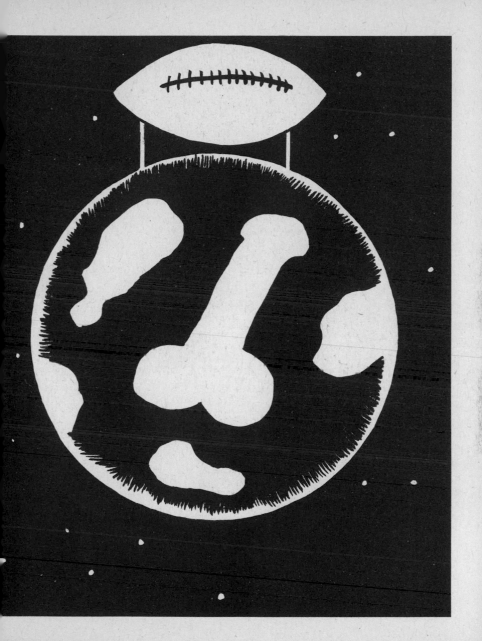

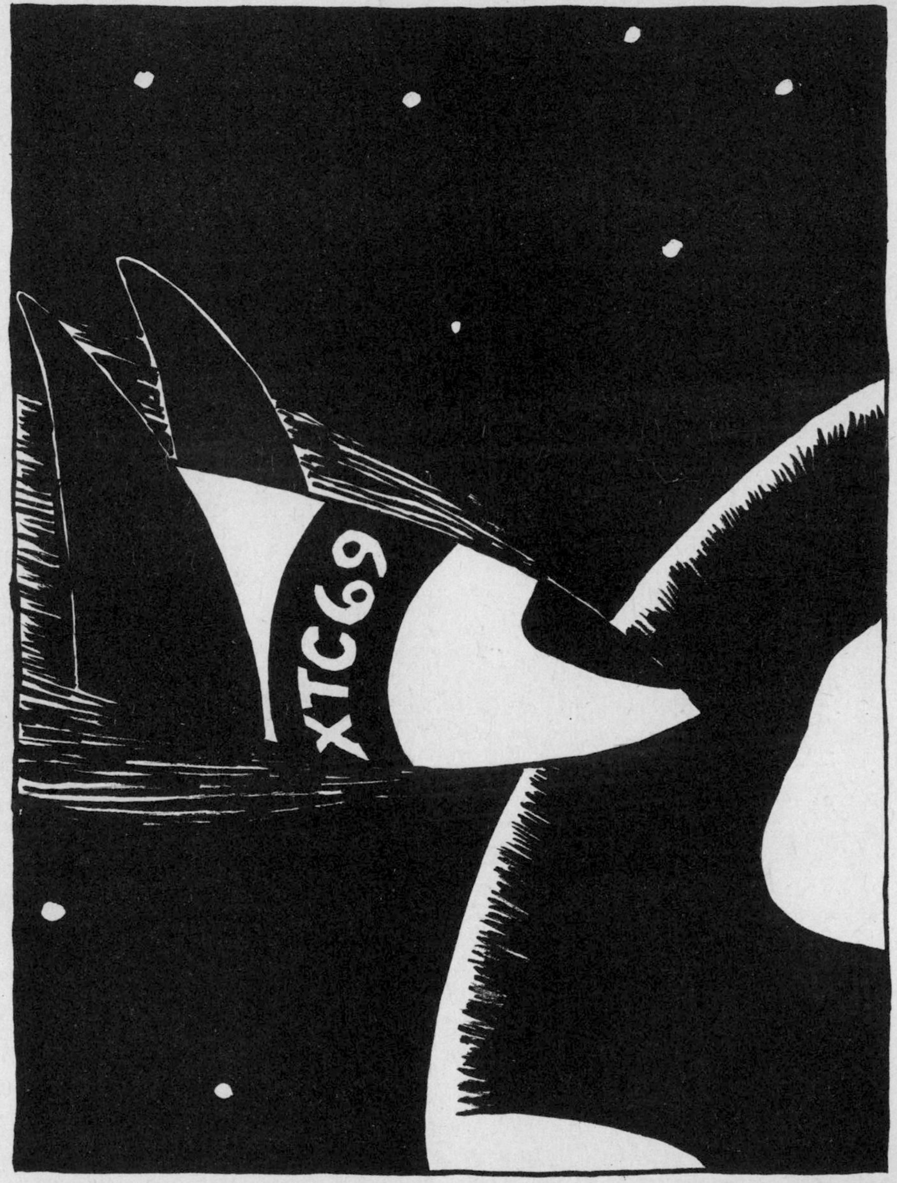
XTC69

CHAPTER 4:
VASTATIO

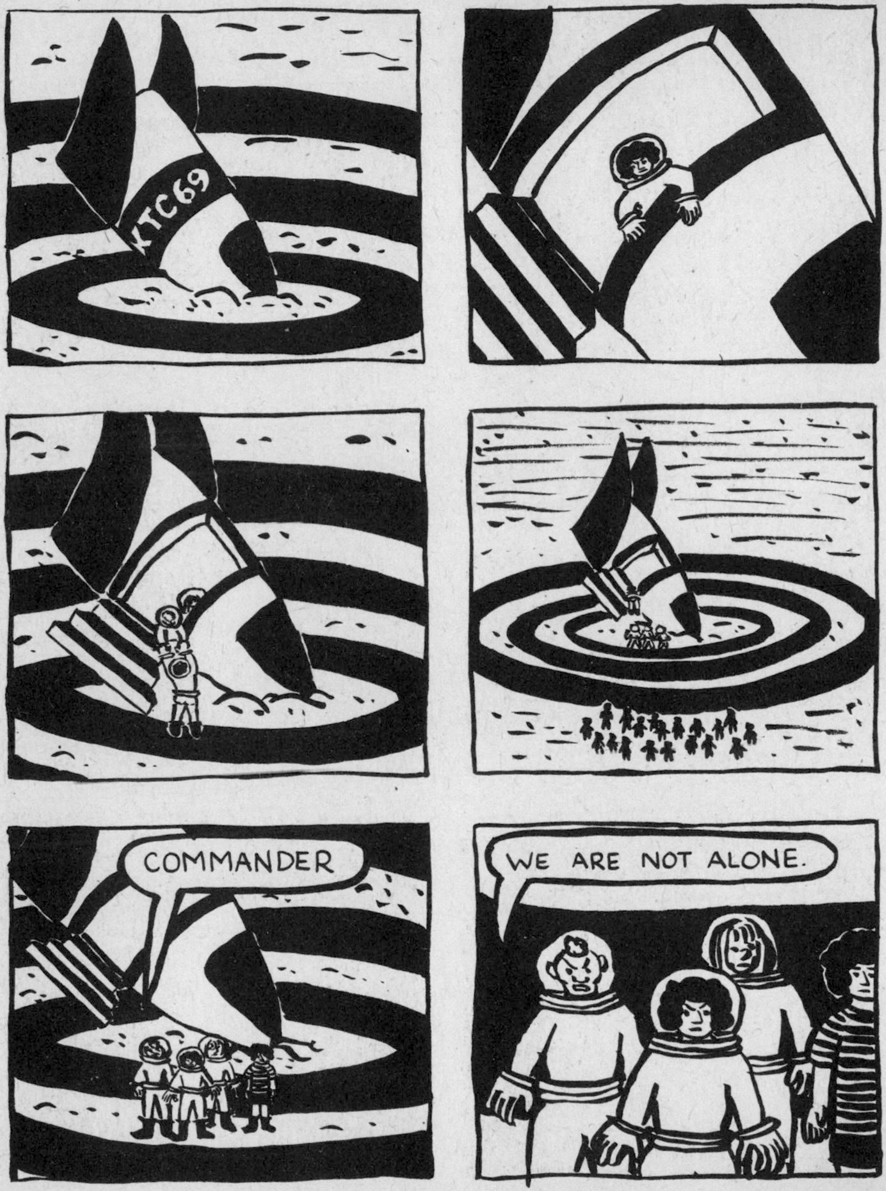
KTC69
COMMANDER
WE ARE NOT ALONE.

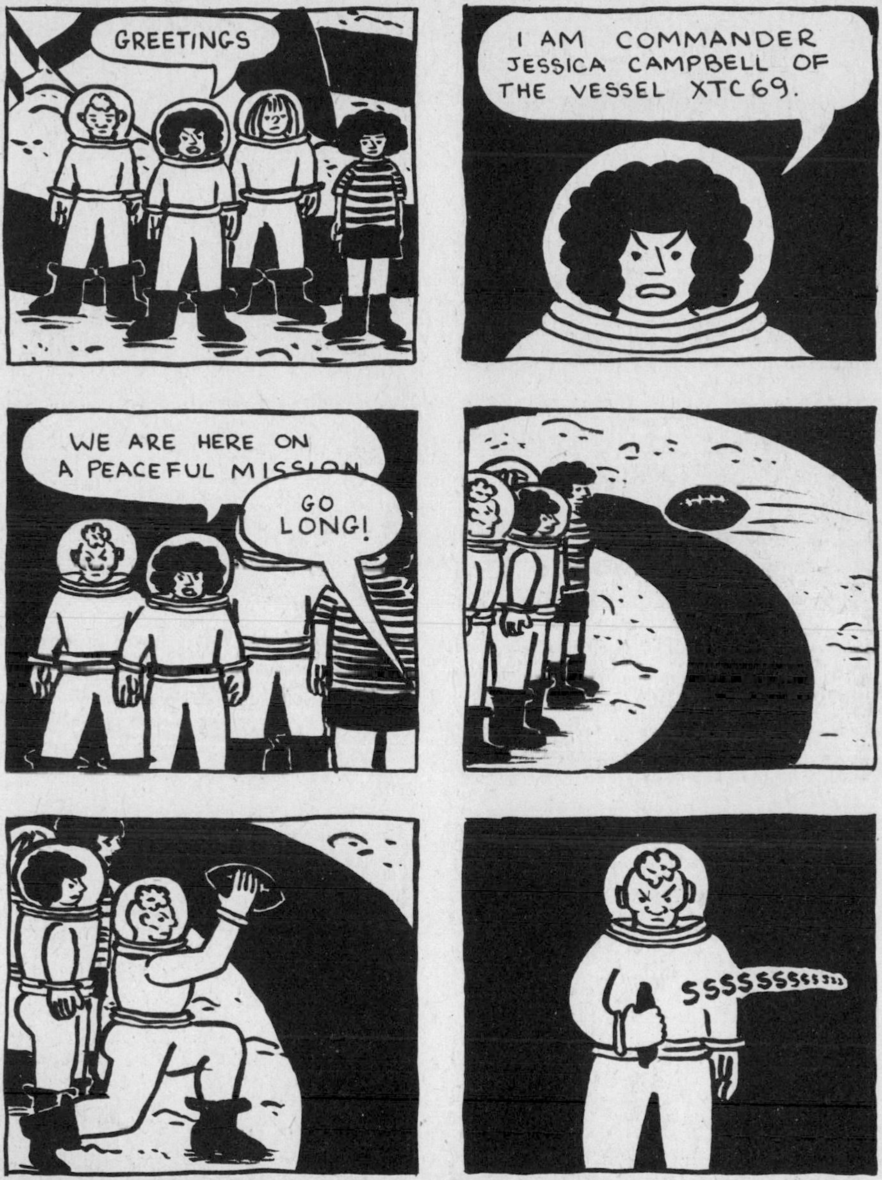
GREETINGS
I AM COMMANDER JESSICA CAMPBELL OF THE VESSEL XTC69.
WE ARE HERE ON A PEACEFUL MISSION
GO LONG!
SSSSSSSsssss

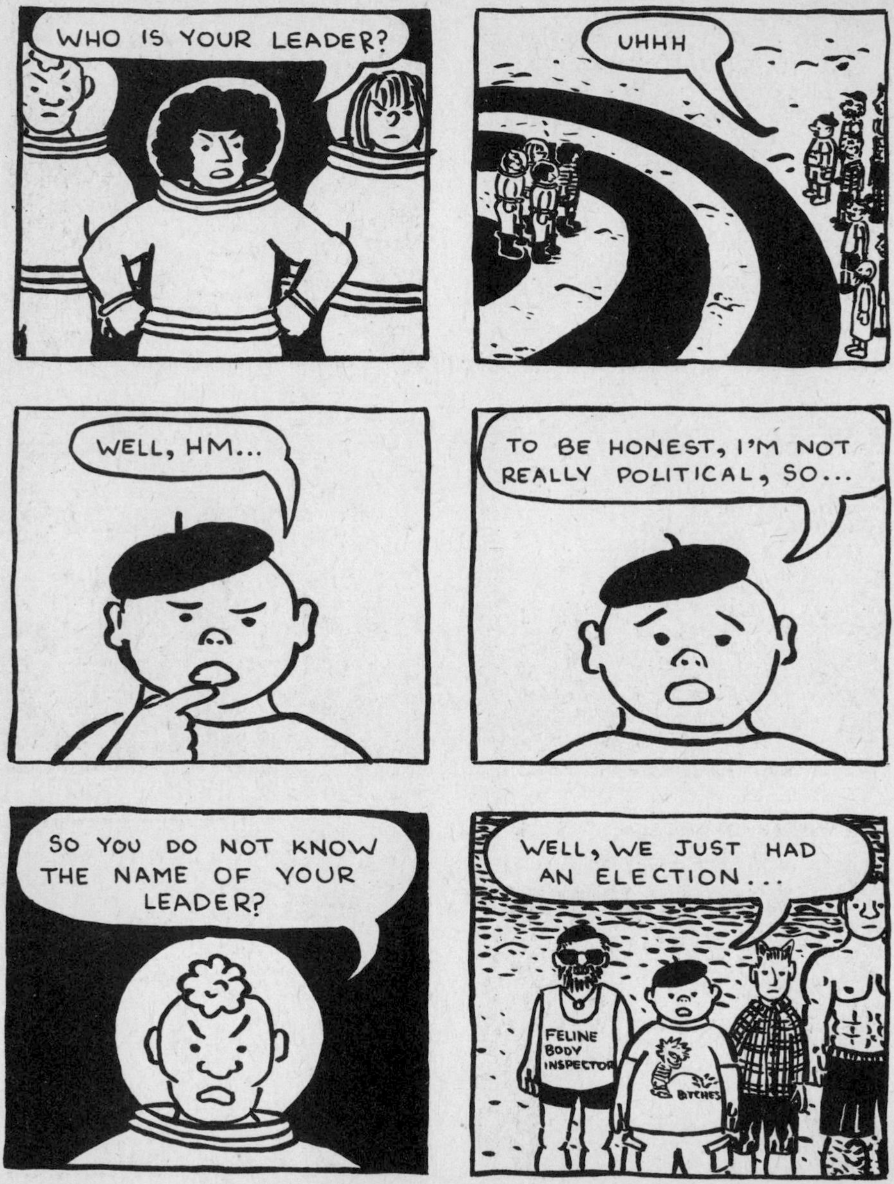
WHO IS YOUR LEADER?
UHHH
WELL, HM...
TO BE HONEST, I'M NOT REALLY POLITICAL, SO...
SO YOU DO NOT KNOW THE NAME OF YOUR LEADER?
WELL, WE JUST HAD AN ELECTION...
FELINE BODY INSPECTOR
BITCHES

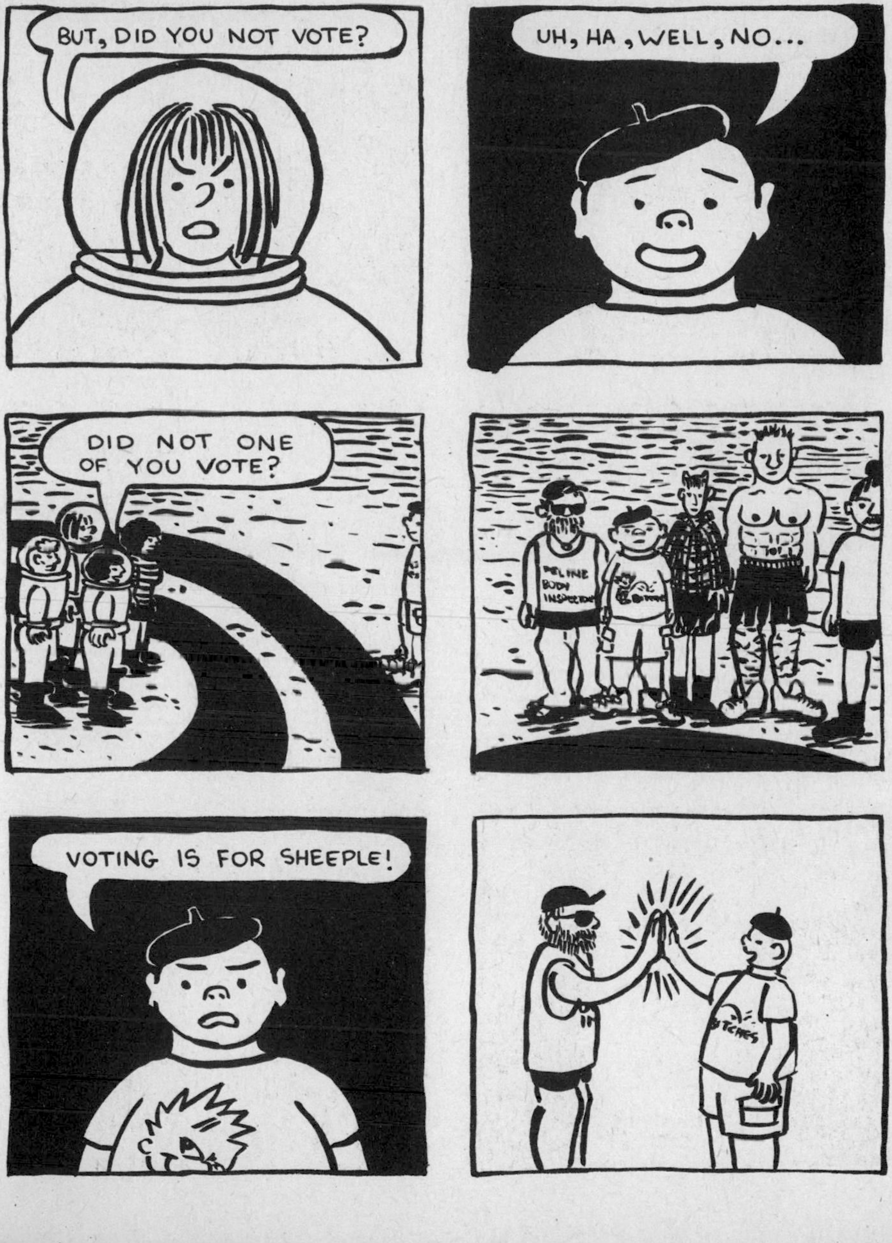
BUT, DID YOU NOT VOTE?
UH, HA, WELL, NO...
DID NOT ONE OF YOU VOTE?
VOTING IS FOR SHEEPLE!

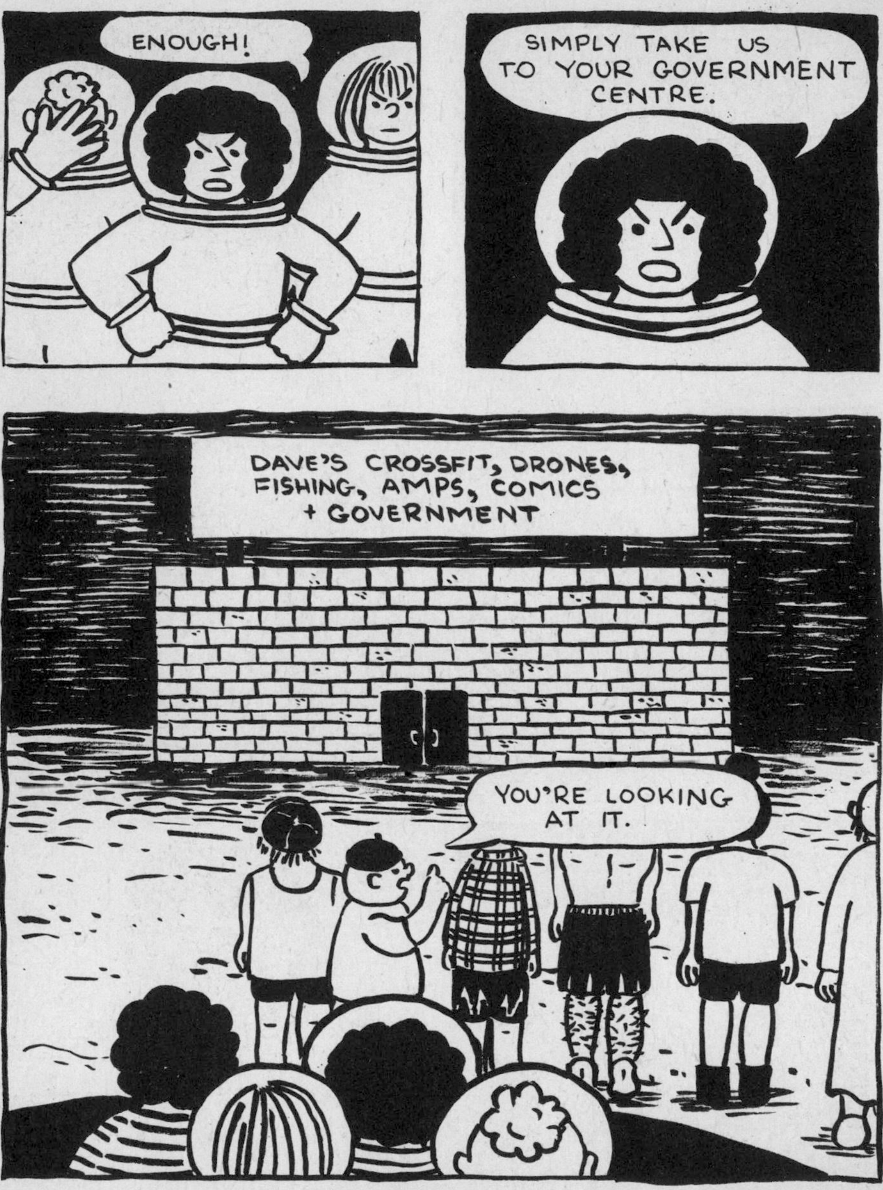
ENOUGH!
SIMPLY TAKE US TO YOUR GOVERNMENT CENTRE.
DAVE'S CROSSFIT, DRONES, FISHING, AMPS, COMICS + GOVERNMENT
YOU'RE LOOKING AT IT.

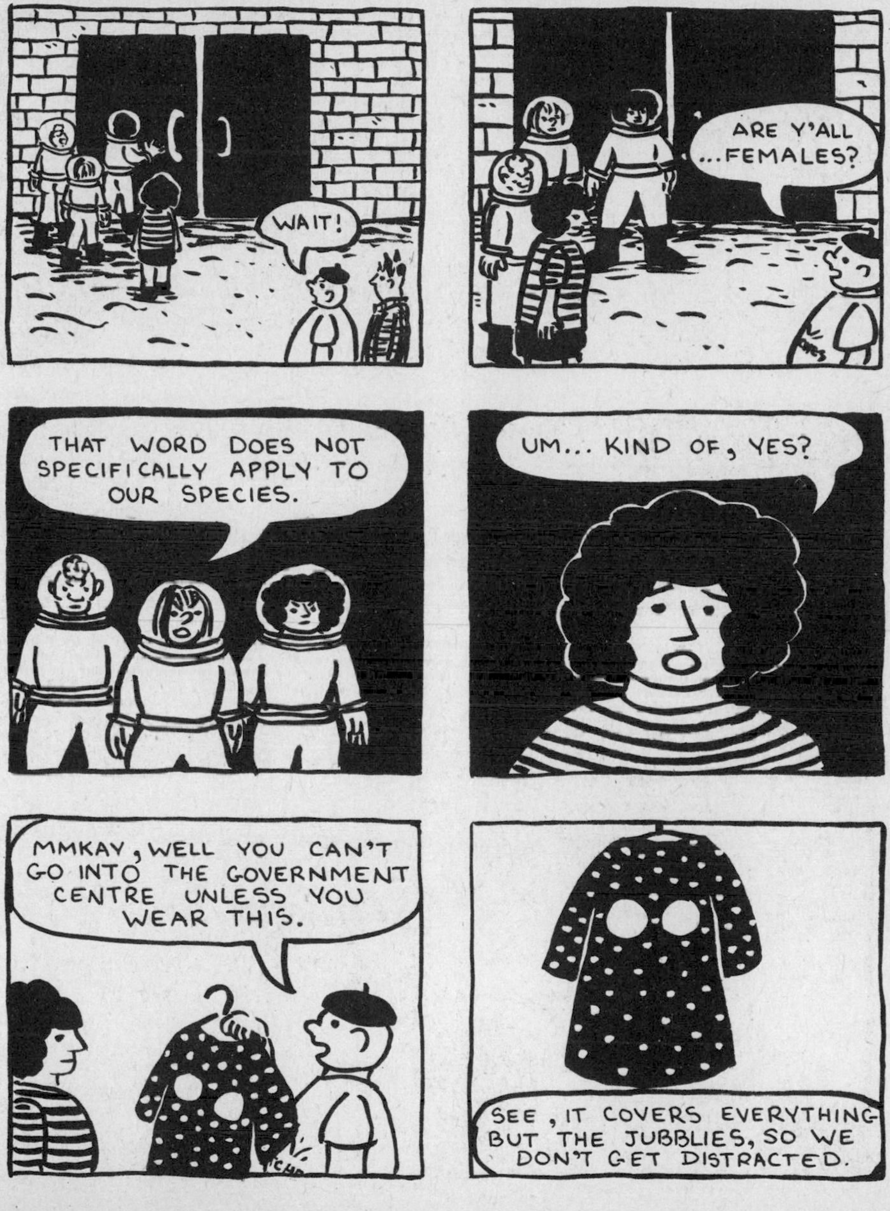
WAIT!
ARE Y'ALL
...FEMALES?
THAT WORD DOES NOT SPECIFICALLY APPLY TO OUR SPECIES.
UM... KIND OF, YES?
MMKAY, WELL YOU CAN'T GO INTO THE GOVERNMENT CENTRE UNLESS YOU WEAR THIS.
SEE, IT COVERS EVERYTHING BUT THE JUBBLIES, SO WE DON'T GET DISTRACTED.

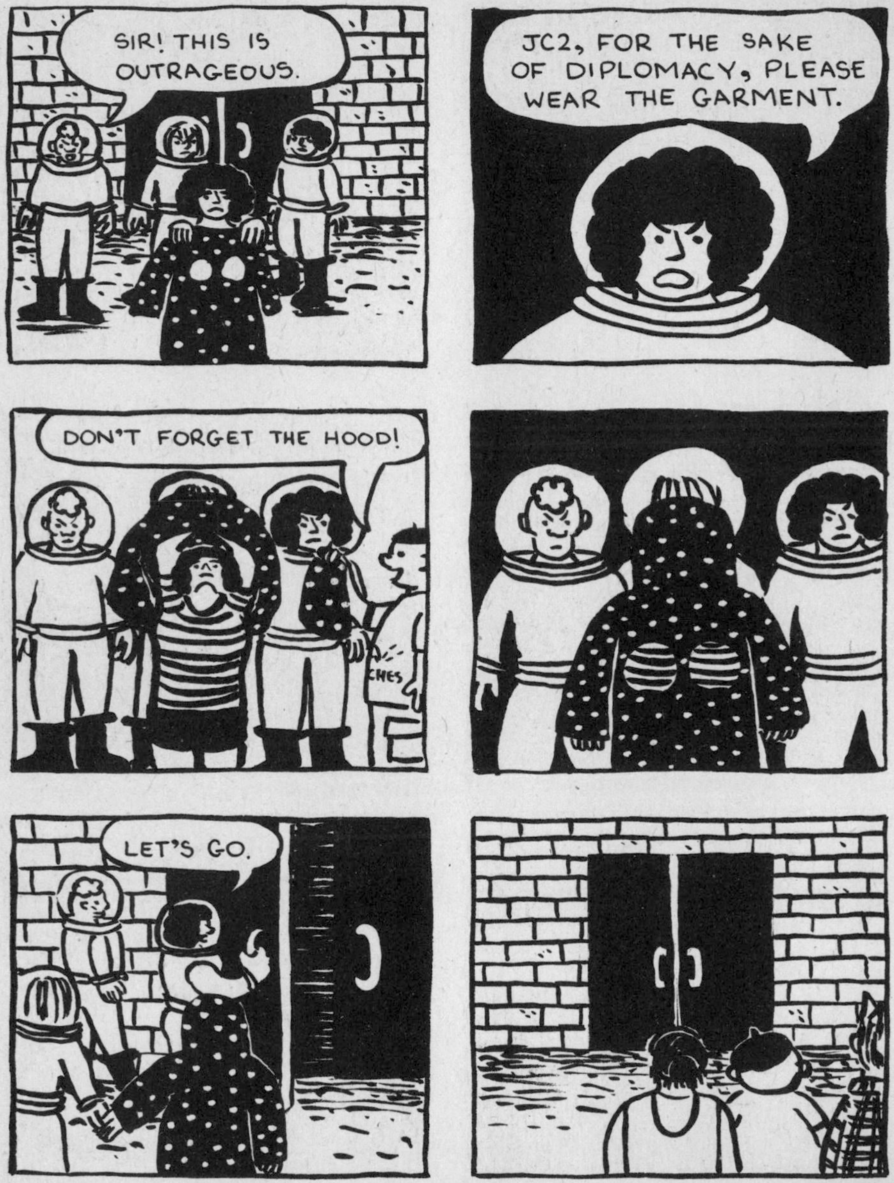
SIR! THIS IS OUTRAGEOUS.
JC2, FOR THE SAKE OF DIPLOMACY, PLEASE WEAR THE GARMENT.
DON'T FORGET THE HOOD!
LET'S GO.

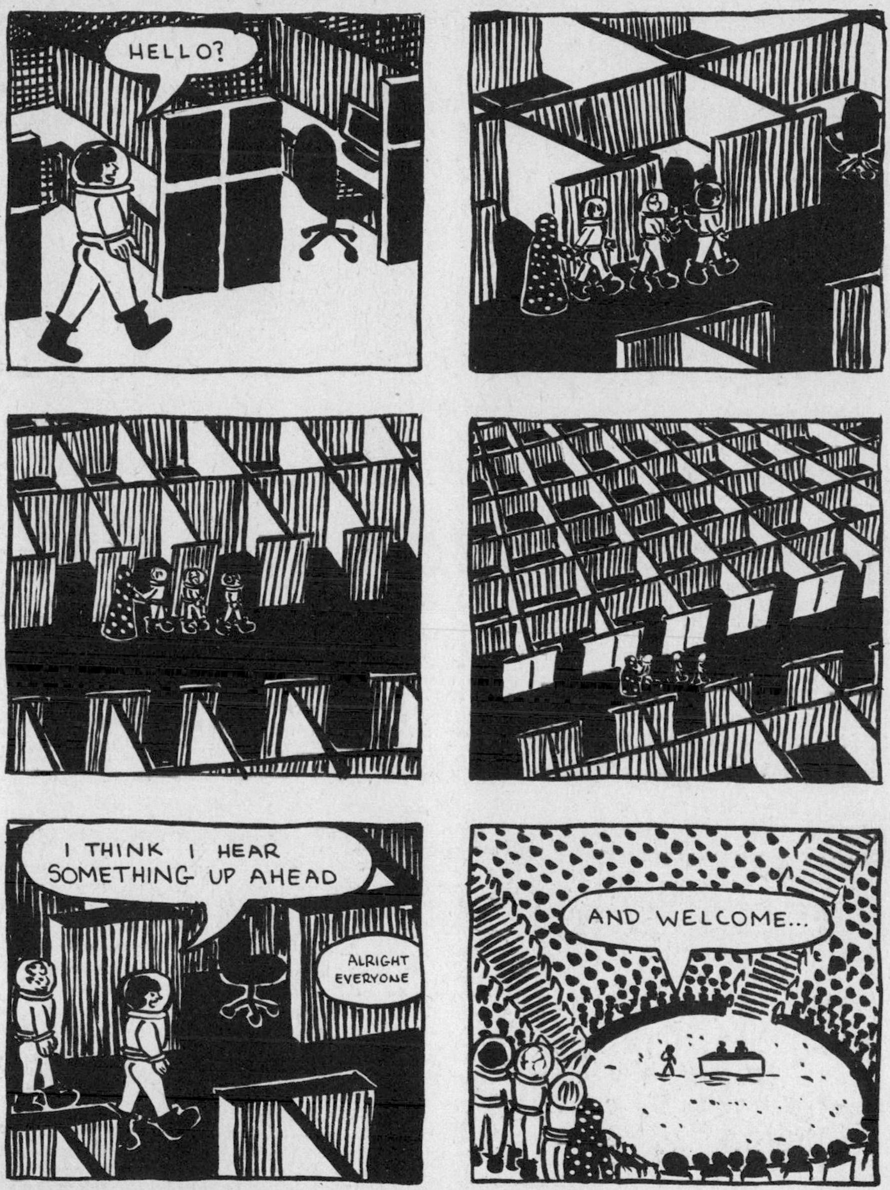
HELLO?
I THINK I HEAR SOMETHING UP AHEAD
ALRIGHT EVERYONE
AND WELCOME...

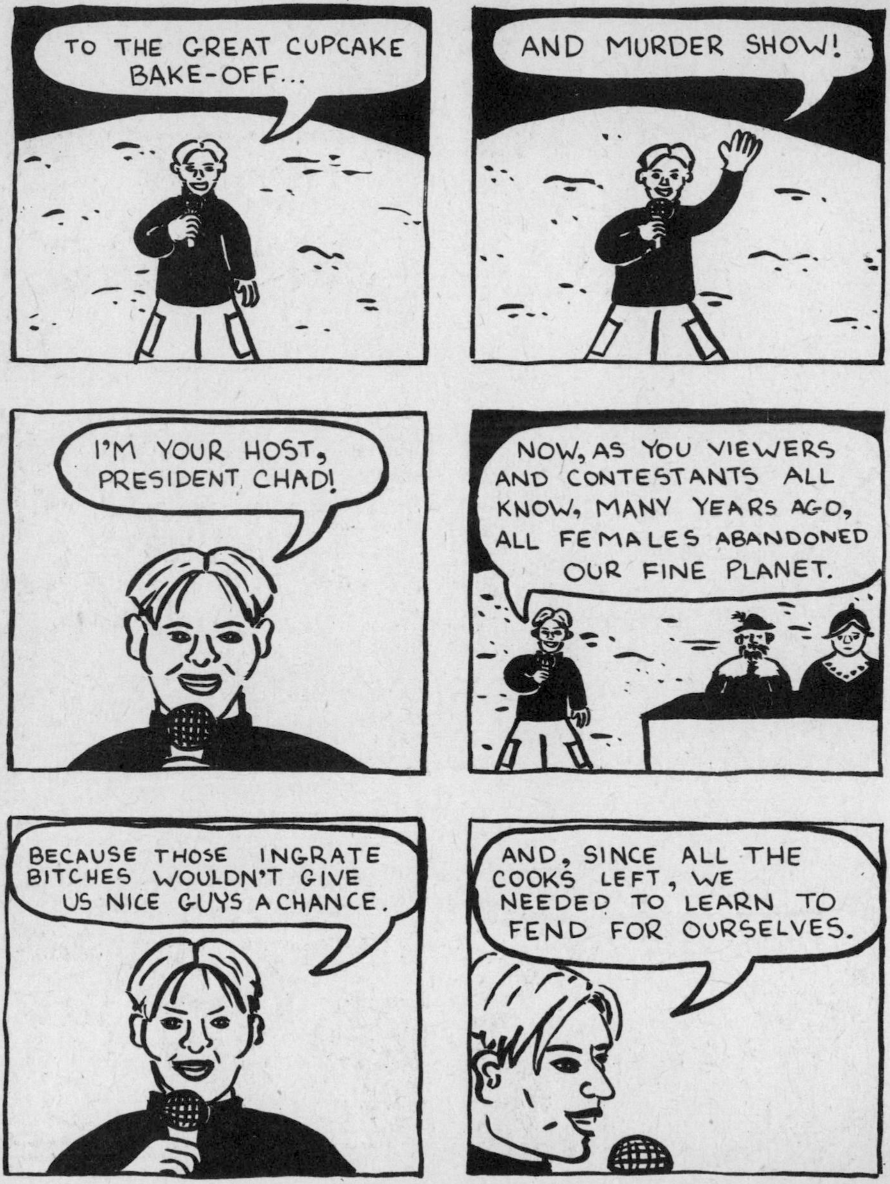

TO THE GREAT CUPCAKE BAKE-OFF...
AND MURDER SHOW!
I'M YOUR HOST, PRESIDENT CHAD!
NOW, AS YOU VIEWERS AND CONTESTANTS ALL KNOW, MANY YEARS AGO, ALL FEMALES ABANDONED OUR FINE PLANET.
BECAUSE THOSE INGRATE BITCHES WOULDN'T GIVE US NICE GUYS A CHANCE.
AND, SINCE ALL THE COOKS LEFT, WE NEEDED TO LEARN TO FEND FOR OURSELVES.

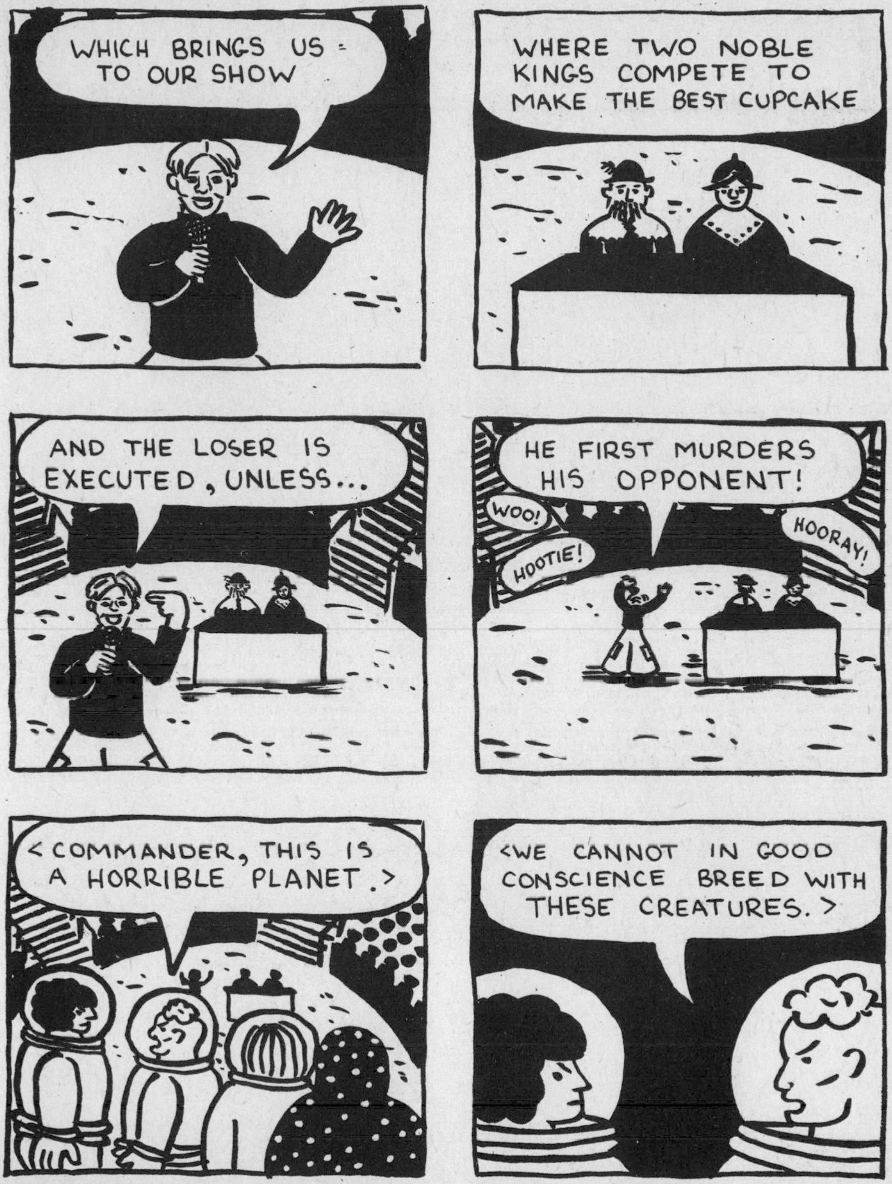
WHICH BRINGS US TO OUR SHOW
WHERE TWO NOBLE KINGS COMPETE TO MAKE THE BEST CUPCAKE
AND THE LOSER IS EXECUTED, UNLESS...
HE FIRST MURDERS HIS OPPONENT!
WOO!
HOOTIE!
HOORAY!
<COMMANDER, THIS IS A HORRIBLE PLANET.>
<WE CANNOT IN GOOD CONSCIENCE BREED WITH THESE CREATURES.>

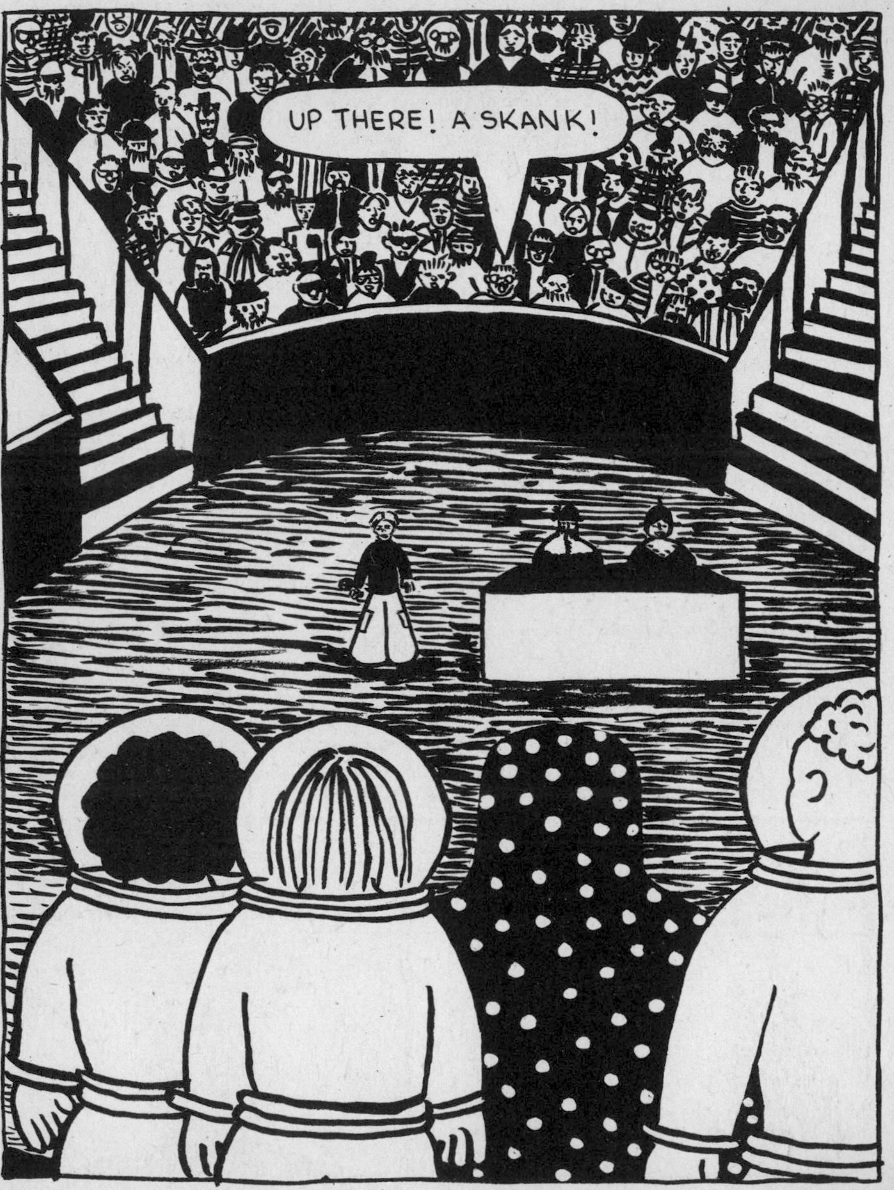
UP THERE! A SKANK!

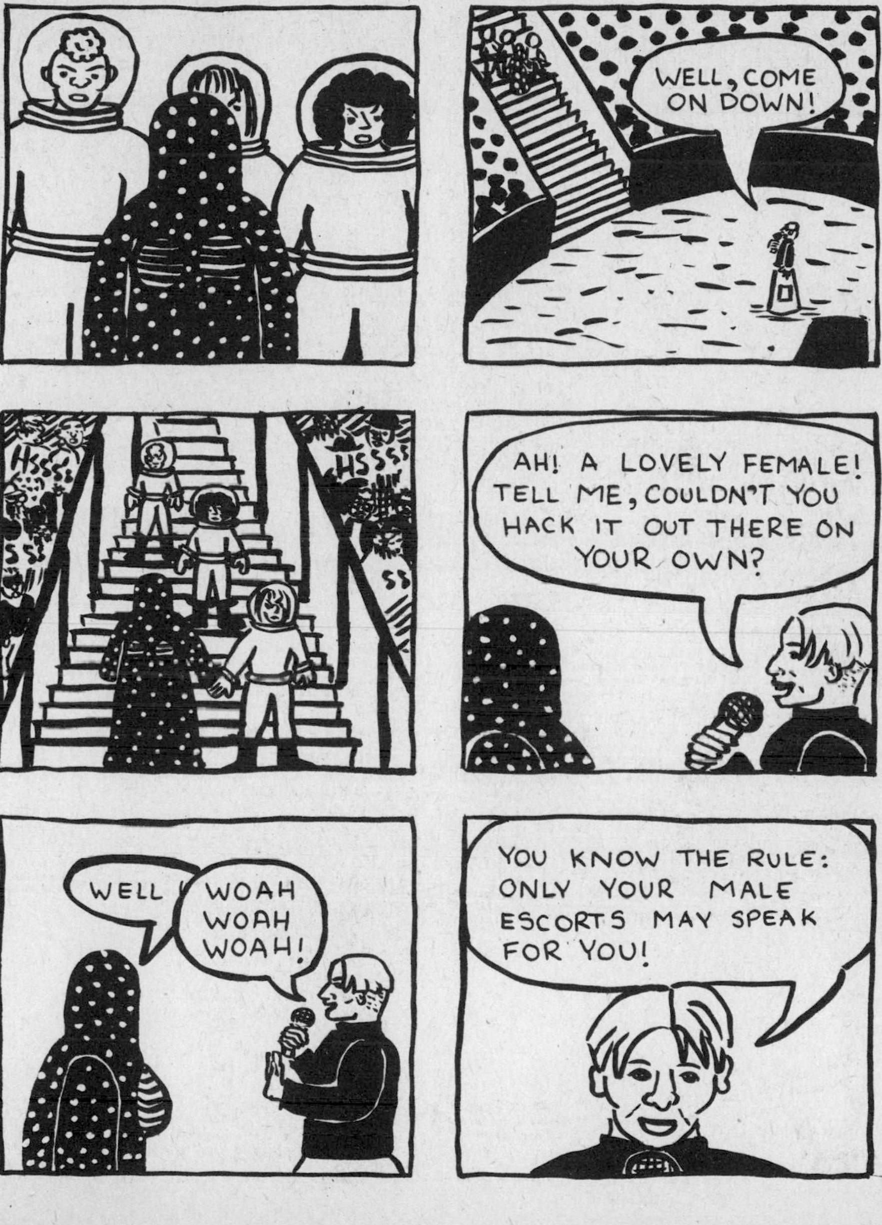
WELL, COME ON DOWN!
HSSSS
HSSSS
SSS
SS
AH! A LOVELY FEMALE! TELL ME, COULDN'T YOU HACK IT OUT THERE ON YOUR OWN?
WELL
WOAH WOAH WOAH!
YOU KNOW THE RULE: ONLY YOUR MALE ESCORTS MAY SPEAK FOR YOU!

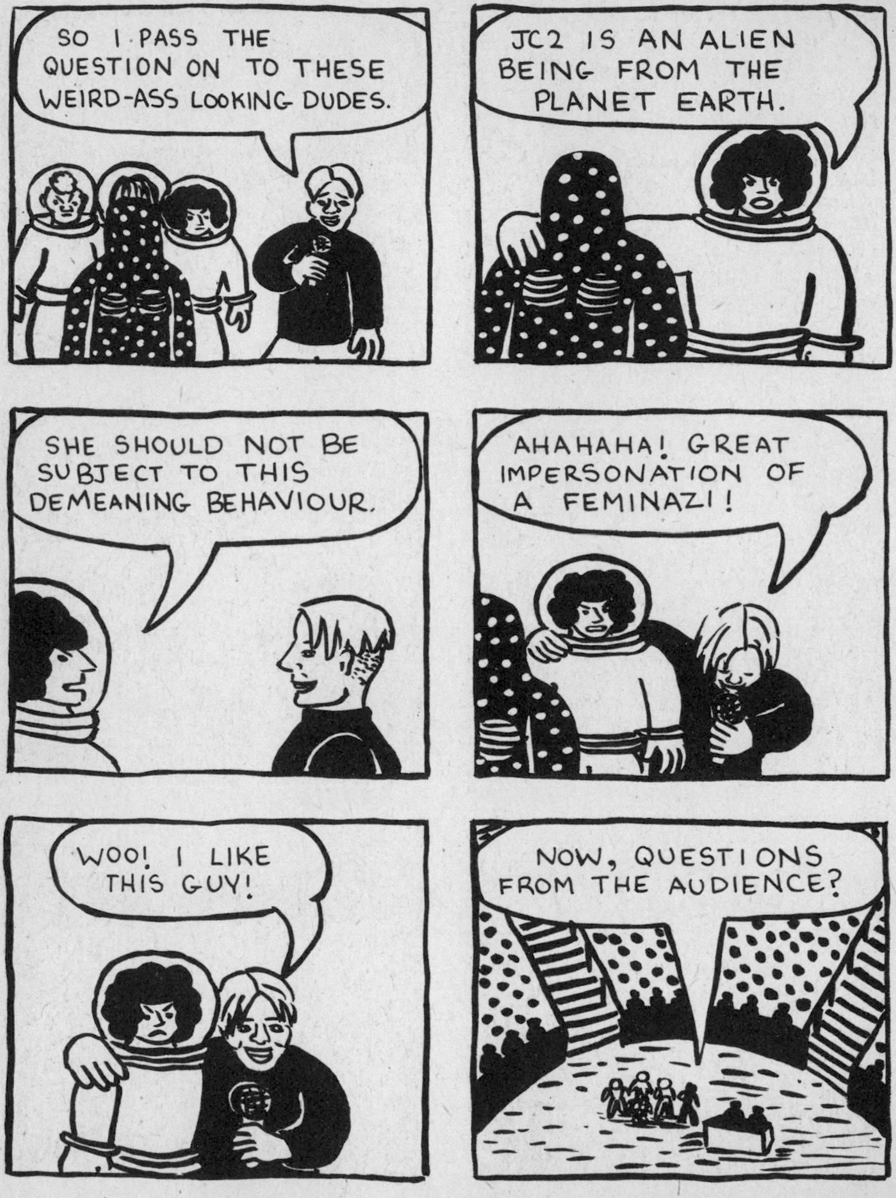
SO I PASS THE QUESTION ON TO THESE WEIRD-ASS LOOKING DUDES.
JC2 IS AN ALIEN BEING FROM THE PLANET EARTH.
SHE SHOULD NOT BE SUBJECT TO THIS DEMEANING BEHAVIOUR.
AHAHAHA! GREAT IMPERSONATION OF A FEMINAZI!
WOO! I LIKE THIS GUY!
NOW, QUESTIONS FROM THE AUDIENCE?

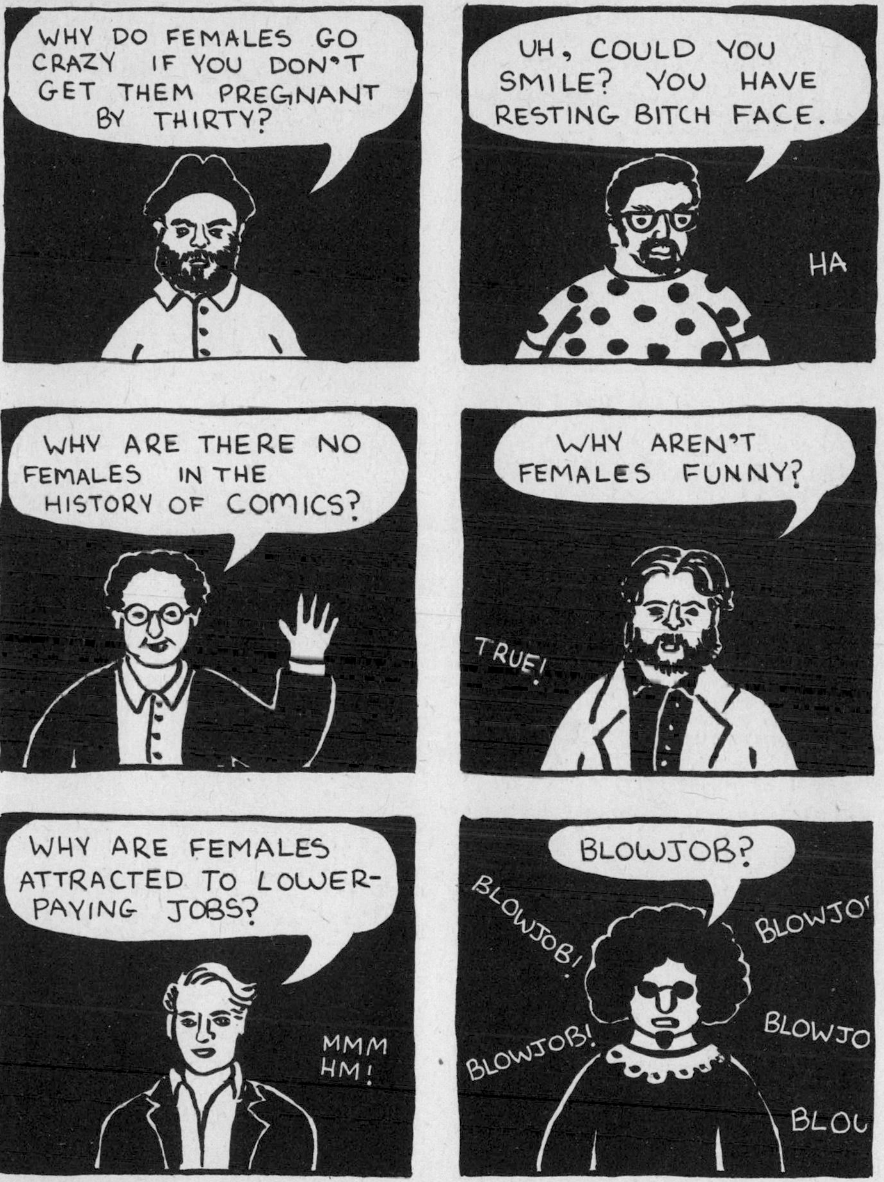
WHY DO FEMALES GO CRAZY IF YOU DON'T GET THEM PREGNANT BY THIRTY?
UH, COULD YOU SMILE? YOU HAVE RESTING BITCH FACE.
HA
WHY ARE THERE NO FEMALES IN THE HISTORY OF COMICS?
WHY AREN'T FEMALES FUNNY?
TRUE!
WHY ARE FEMALES ATTRACTED TO LOWER-PAYING JOBS?
MMM HM!
BLOWJOB?
BLOWJOB!
BLOWJOB!
BLOWJO
BLOWJO
BLOW

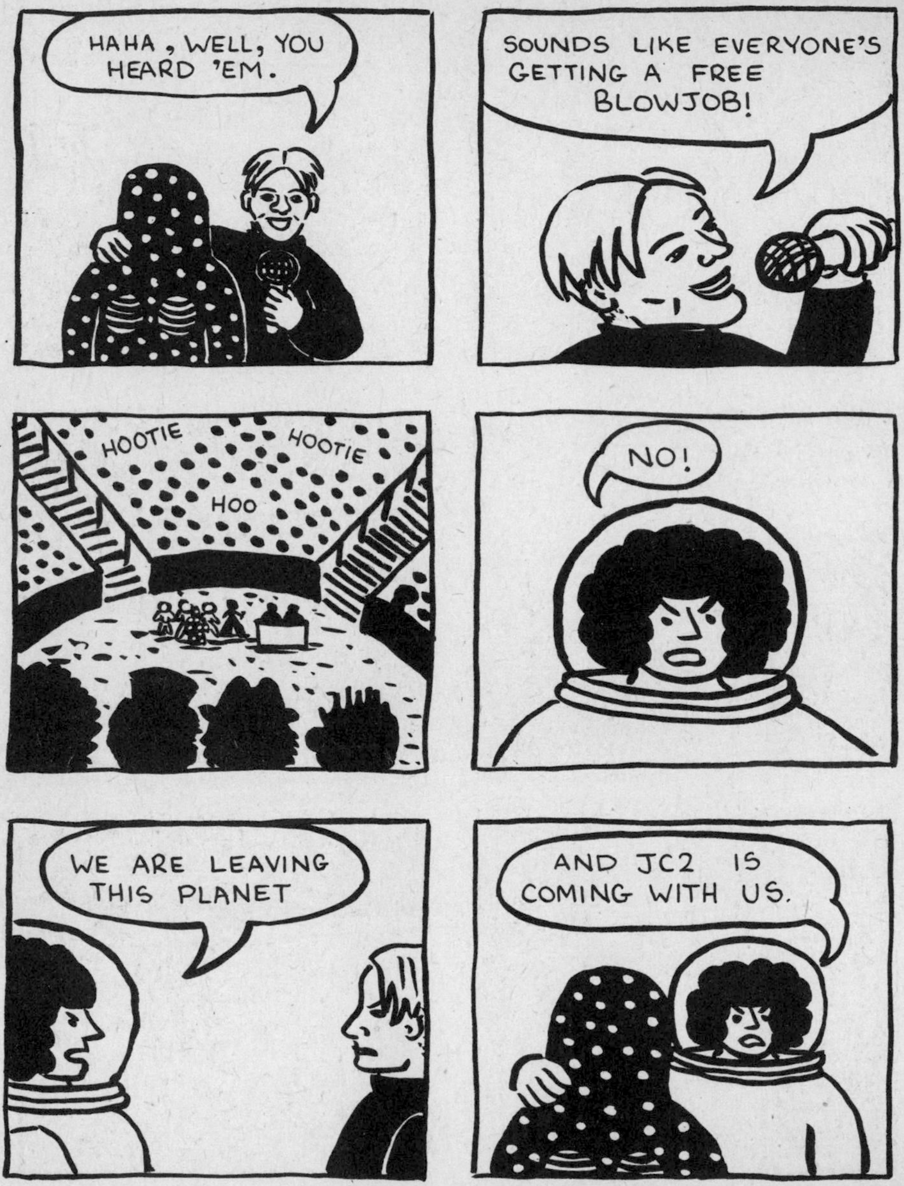
HAHA, WELL, YOU HEARD 'EM.
SOUNDS LIKE EVERYONE'S GETTING A FREE BLOWJOB!
HOOTIE
HOOTIE
HOO
NO!
WE ARE LEAVING THIS PLANET
AND JC2 IS COMING WITH US.

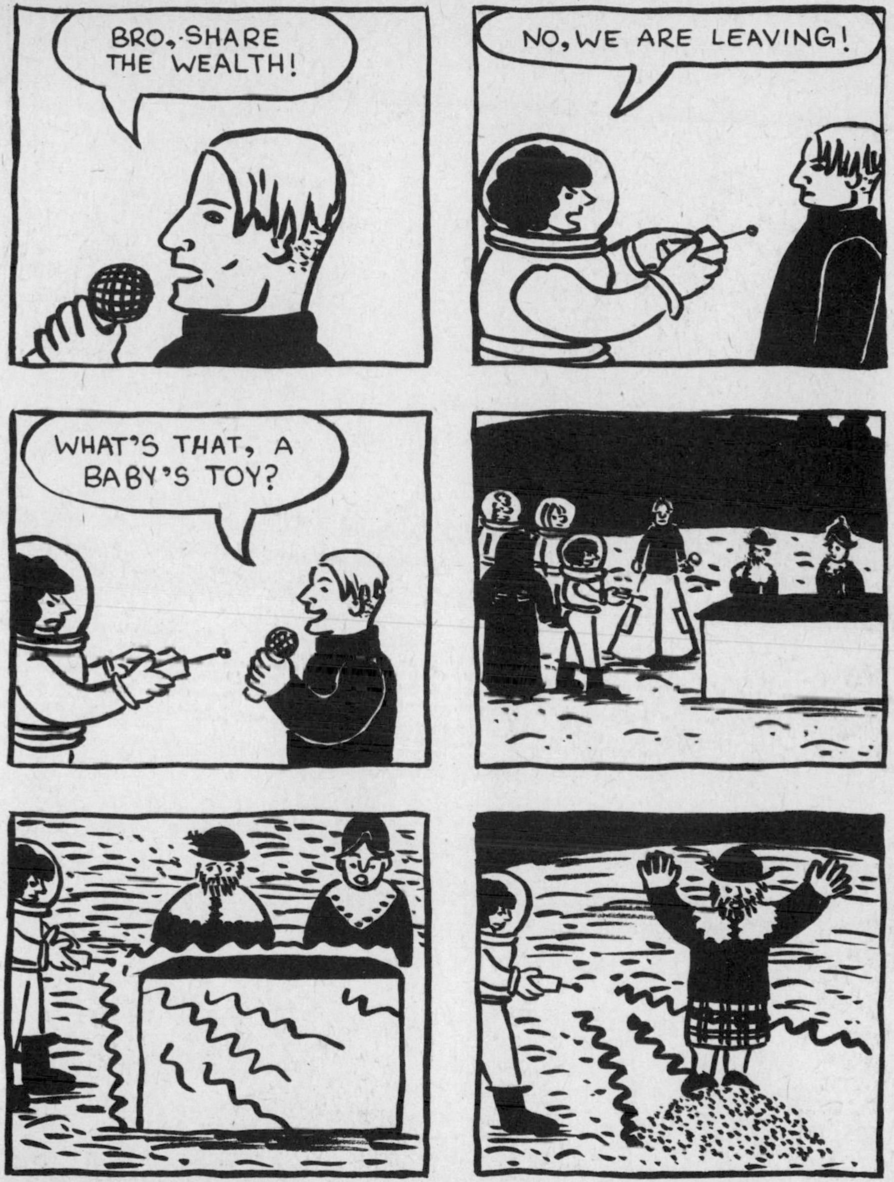
BRO, SHARE THE WEALTH!
NO, WE ARE LEAVING!
WHAT'S THAT, A BABY'S TOY?

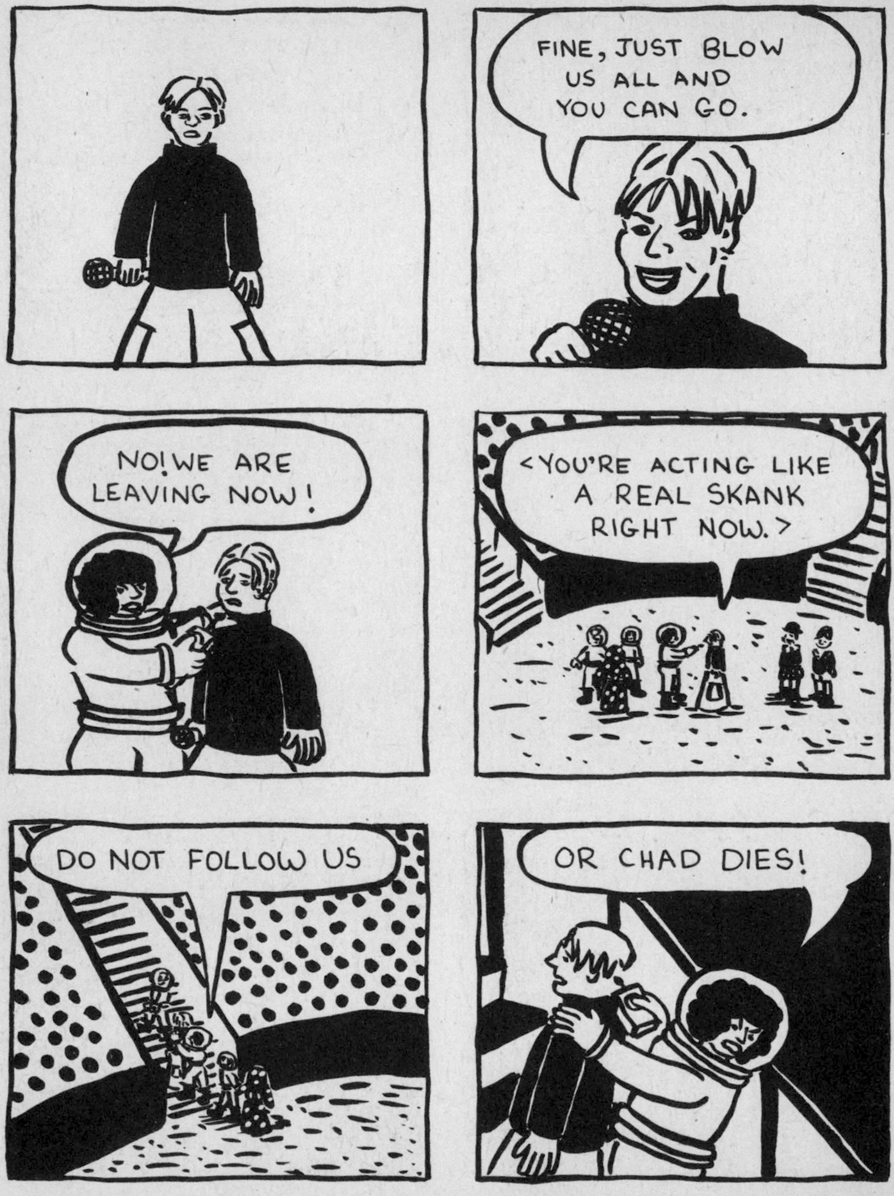

FINE, JUST BLOW US ALL AND YOU CAN GO.
NO! WE ARE LEAVING NOW!
<YOU'RE ACTING LIKE A REAL SKANK RIGHT NOW.>
DO NOT FOLLOW US
OR CHAD DIES!

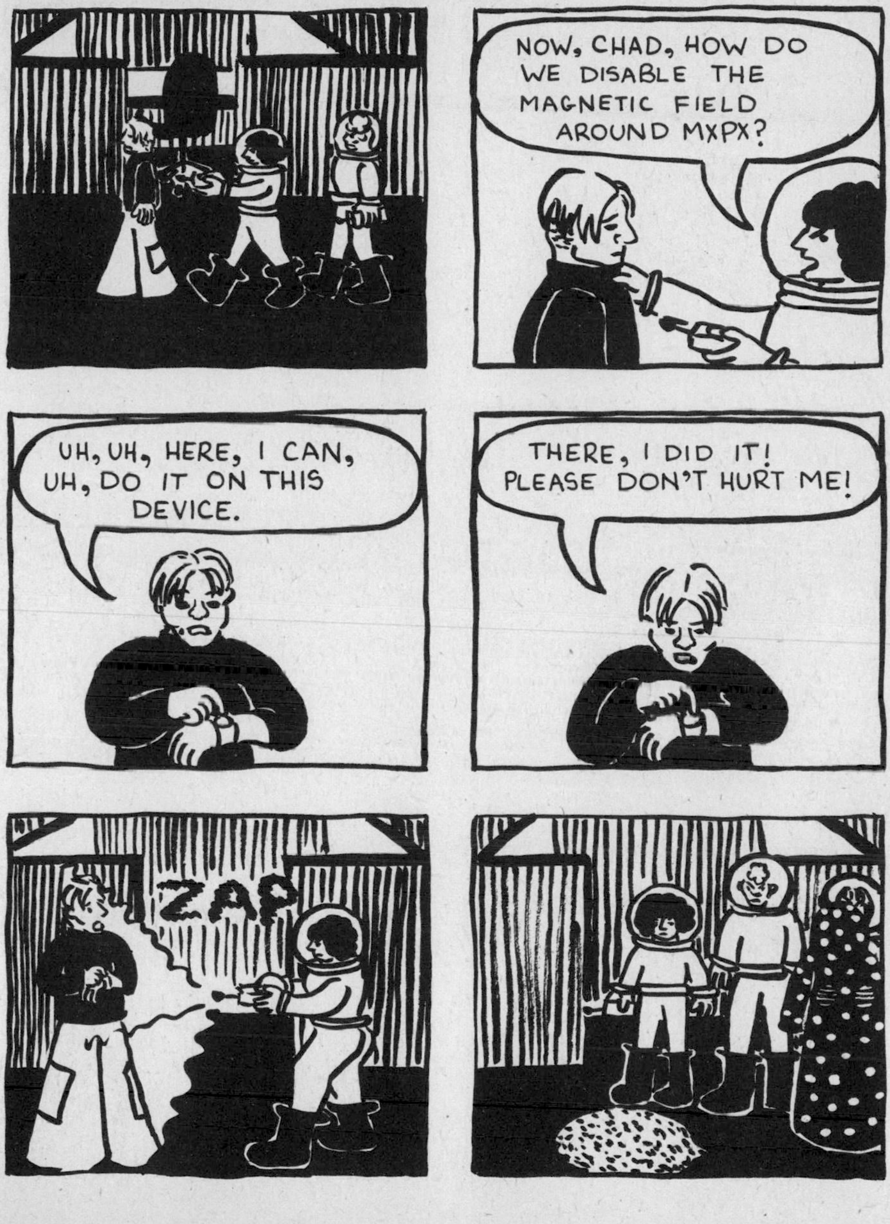
NOW, CHAD, HOW DO WE DISABLE THE MAGNETIC FIELD AROUND MXPX?
UH, UH, HERE, I CAN, UH, DO IT ON THIS DEVICE.
THERE, I DID IT! PLEASE DON'T HURT ME!
ZAP

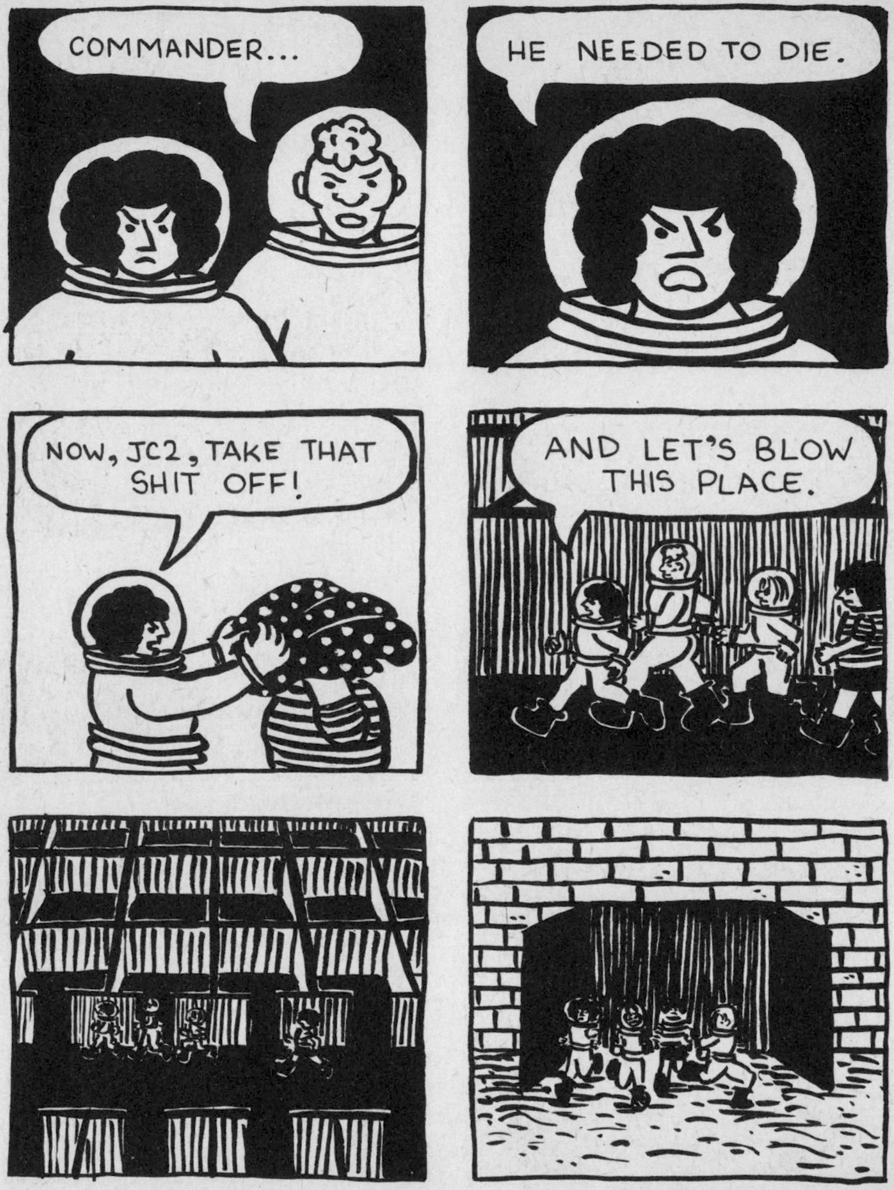
COMMANDER...
HE NEEDED TO DIE.
NOW, JC2, TAKE THAT SHIT OFF!
AND LET'S BLOW THIS PLACE.

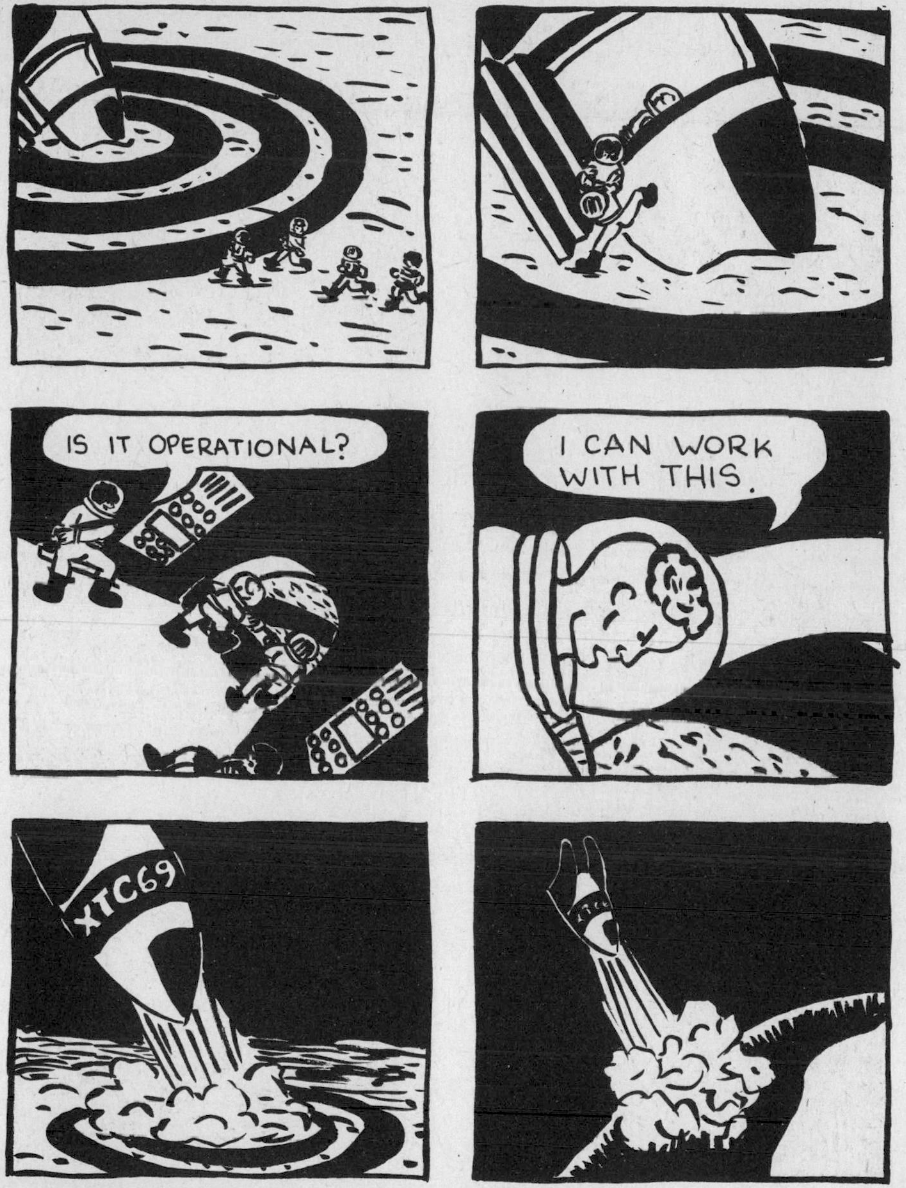
IS IT OPERATIONAL?
I CAN WORK WITH THIS.
XTC69

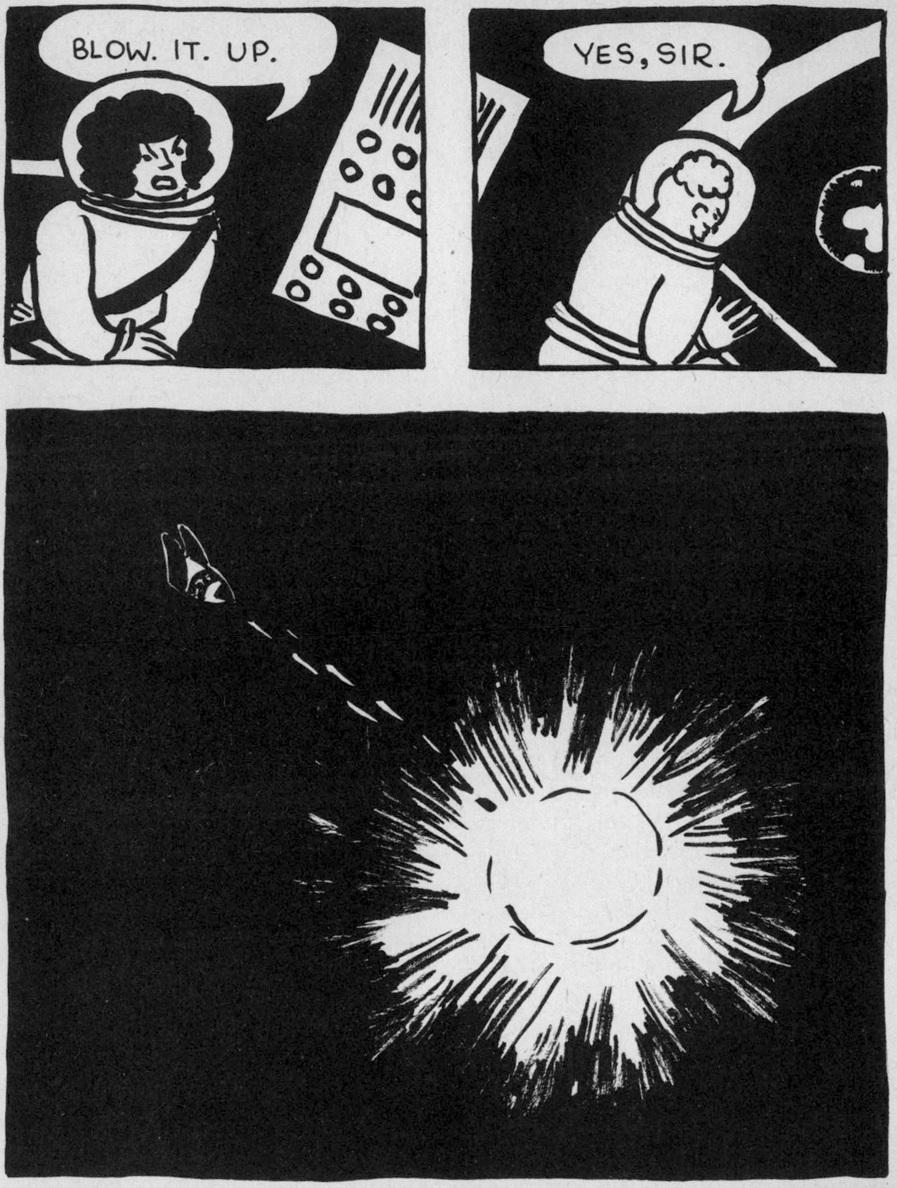
BLOW. IT. UP.
YES, SIR.

CHAPTER 5:
VIGILANS NON CADIT

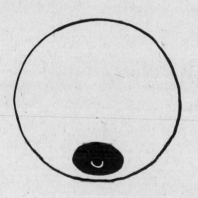

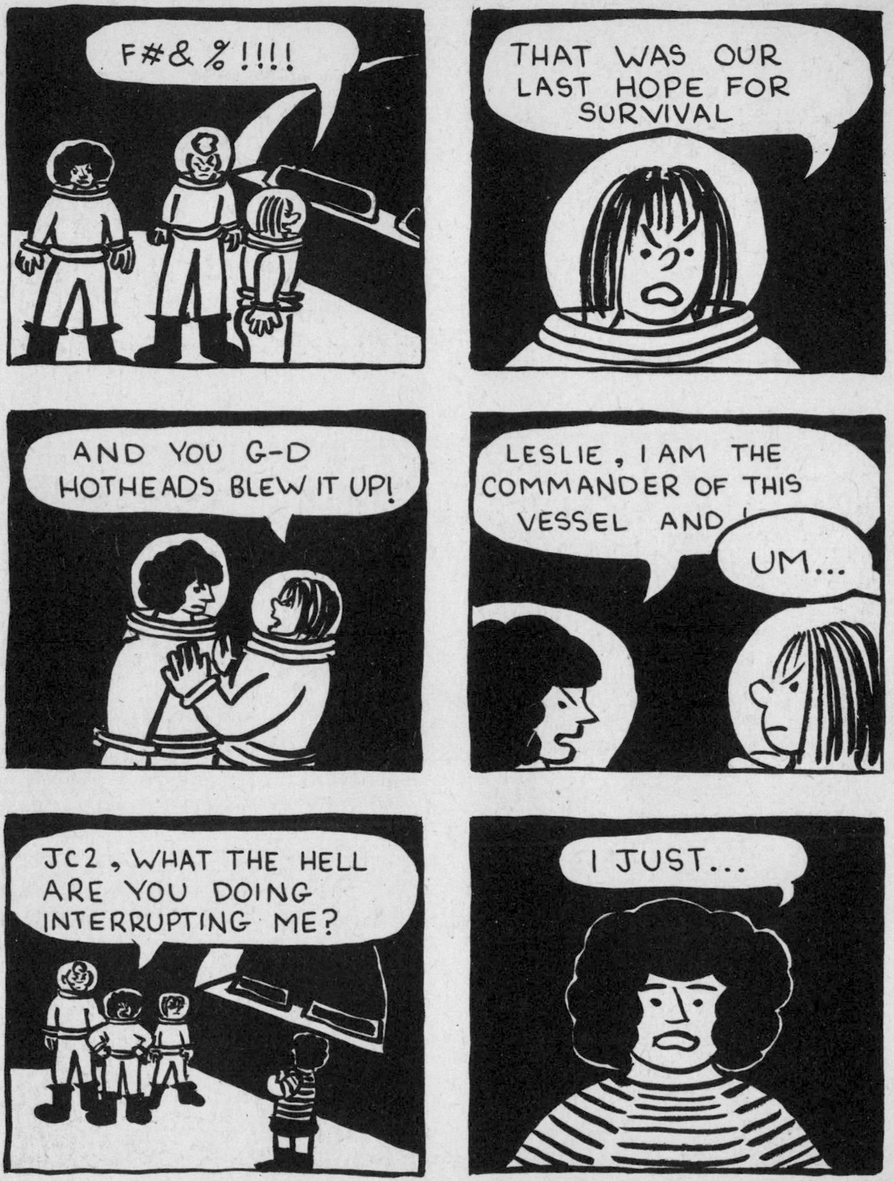
F#&%!!!!
THAT WAS OUR LAST HOPE FOR SURVIVAL
AND YOU G-D HOTHEADS BLEW IT UP!
LESLIE, I AM THE COMMANDER OF THIS VESSEL AND I
UM...
JC2, WHAT THE HELL ARE YOU DOING INTERRUPTING ME?
I JUST...

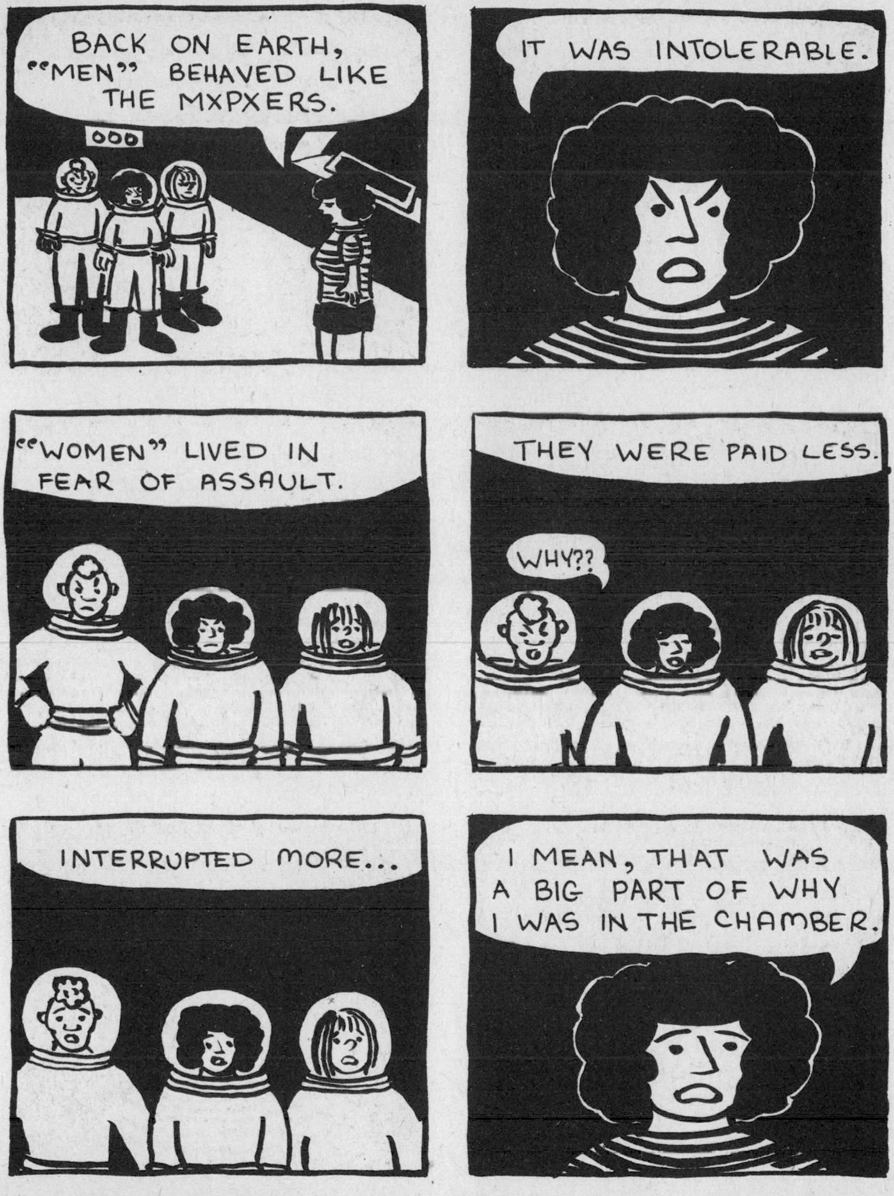

BACK ON EARTH, "MEN" BEHAVED LIKE THE MXPXERS.
OOO
IT WAS INTOLERABLE.
"WOMEN" LIVED IN FEAR OF ASSAULT.
THEY WERE PAID LESS.
WHY??
INTERRUPTED MORE...
I MEAN, THAT WAS A BIG PART OF WHY I WAS IN THE CHAMBER.

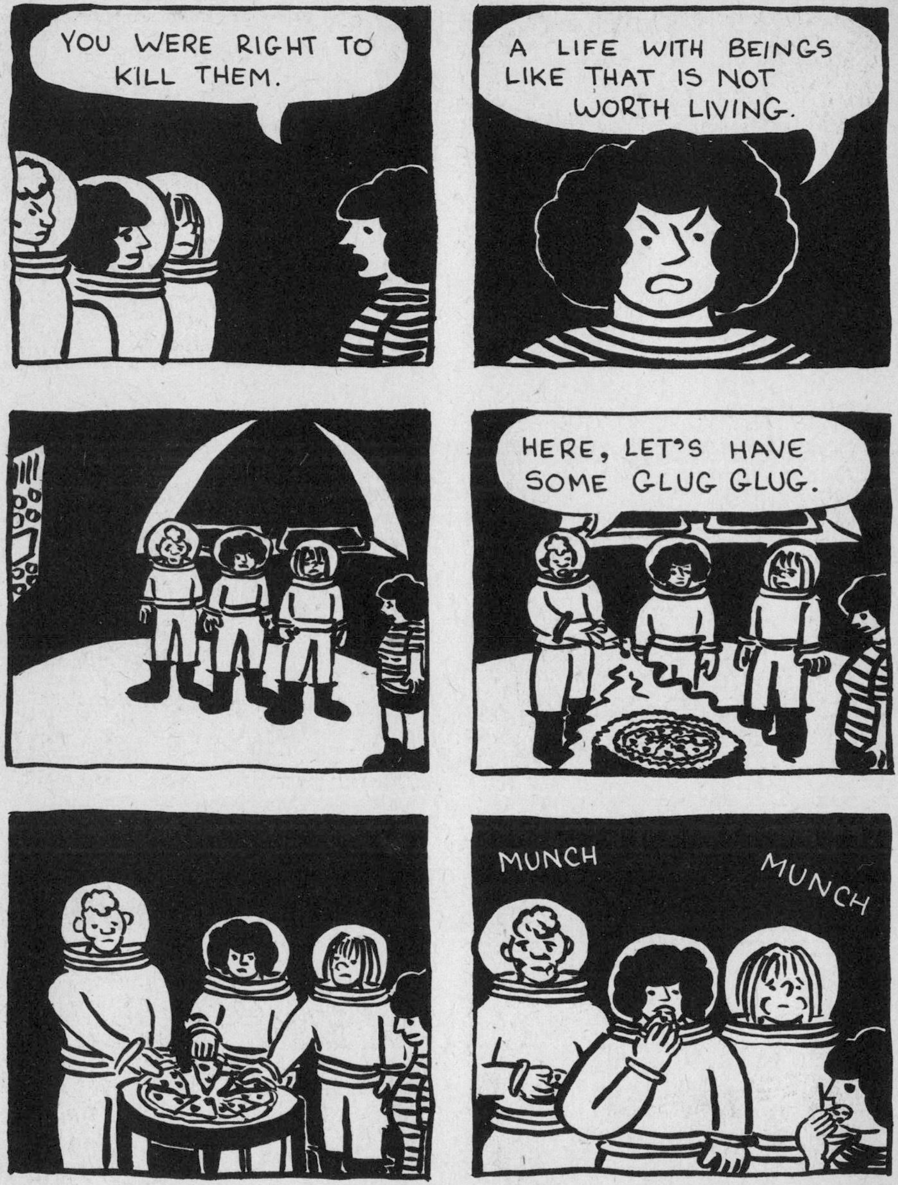
YOU WERE RIGHT TO KILL THEM.
A LIFE WITH BEINGS LIKE THAT IS NOT WORTH LIVING.
HERE, LET'S HAVE SOME GLUG GLUG.
MUNCH
MUNCH

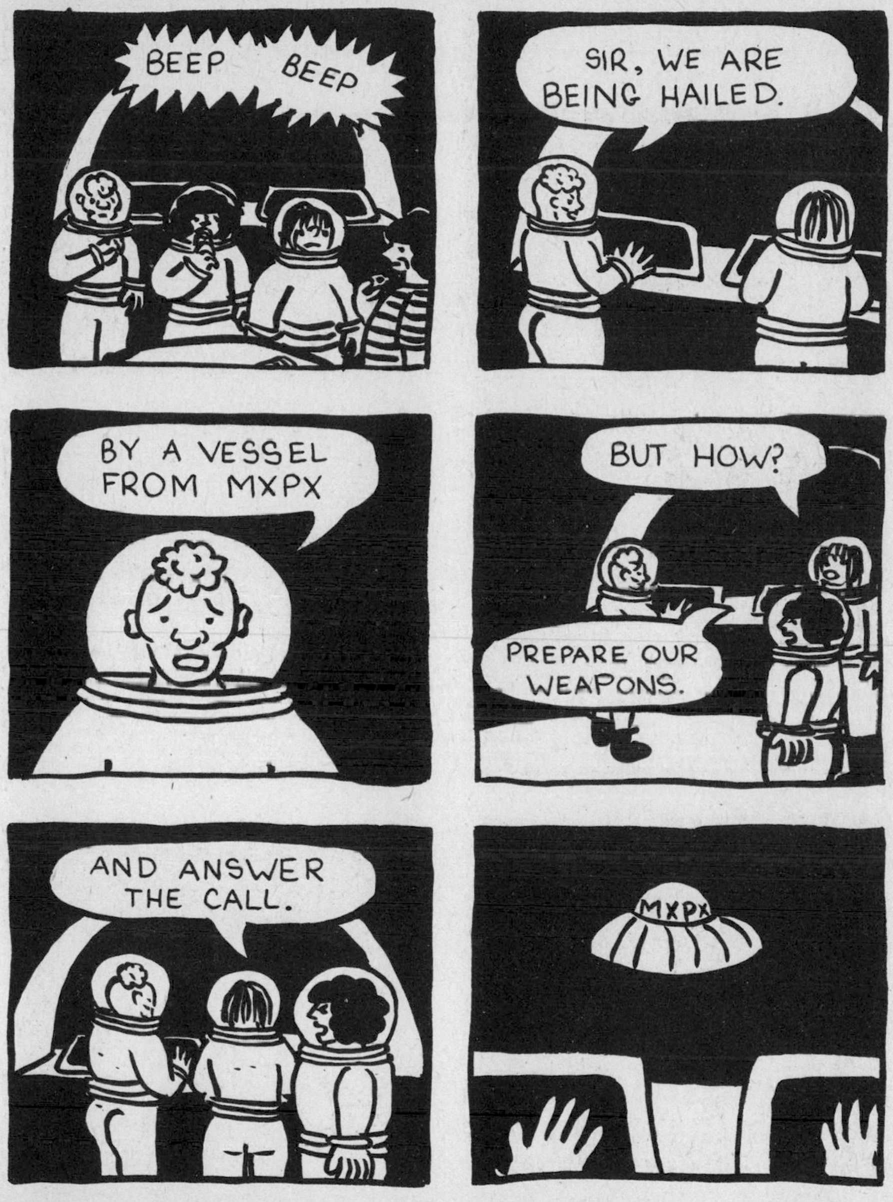
BEEP BEEP
SIR, WE ARE BEING HAILED.
BY A VESSEL FROM MXPX
BUT HOW?
PREPARE OUR WEAPONS.
AND ANSWER THE CALL.
MXPX

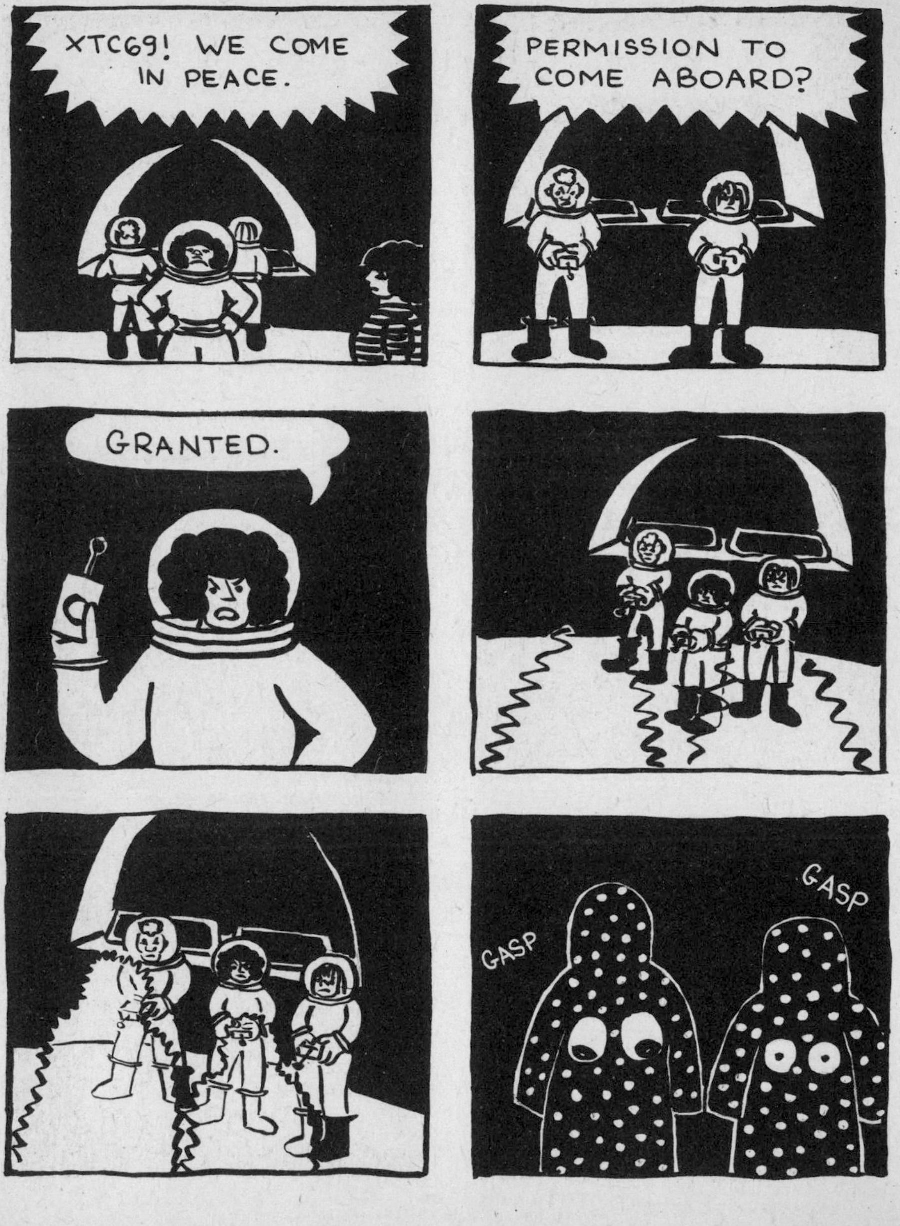
XTC69! WE COME IN PEACE.
PERMISSION TO COME ABOARD?
GRANTED.
GASP
GASP

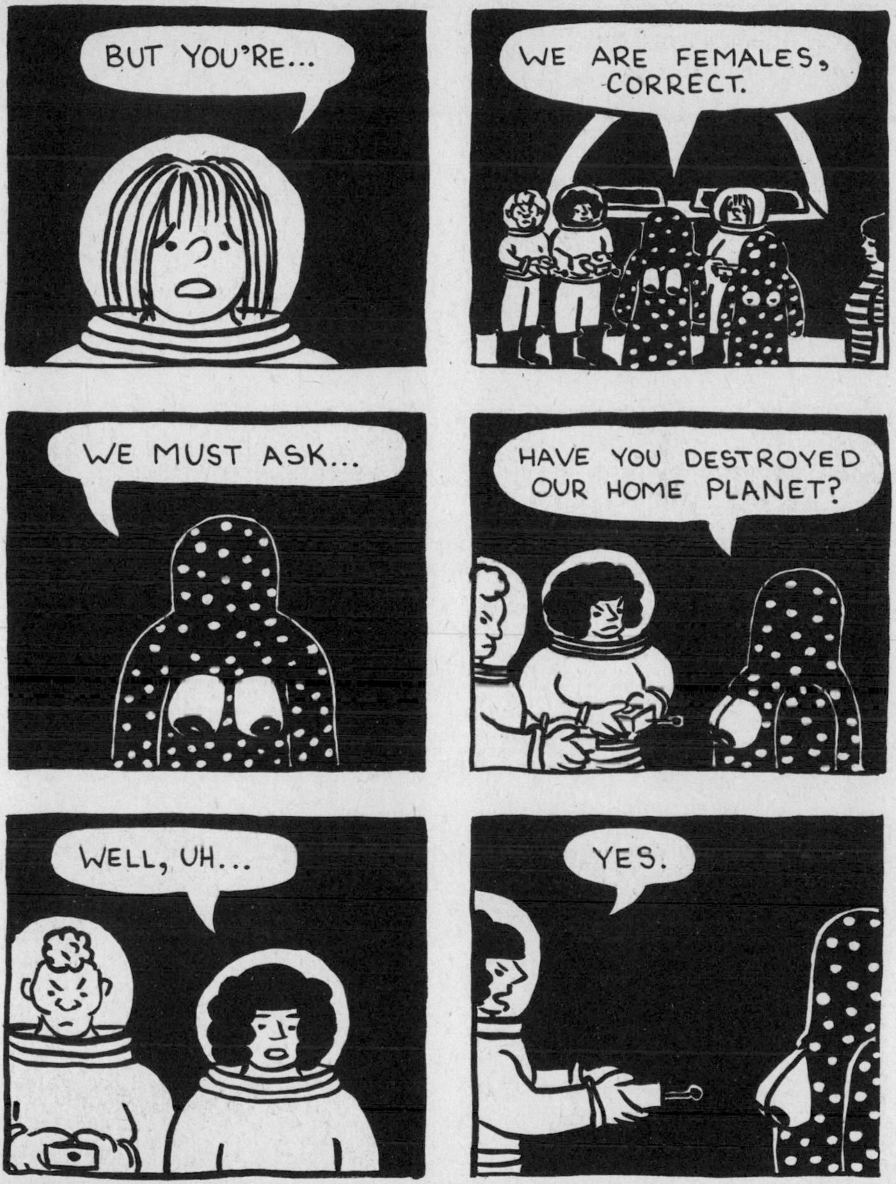
BUT YOU'RE...
WE ARE FEMALES, CORRECT.
WE MUST ASK...
HAVE YOU DESTROYED OUR HOME PLANET?
WELL, UH...
YES.

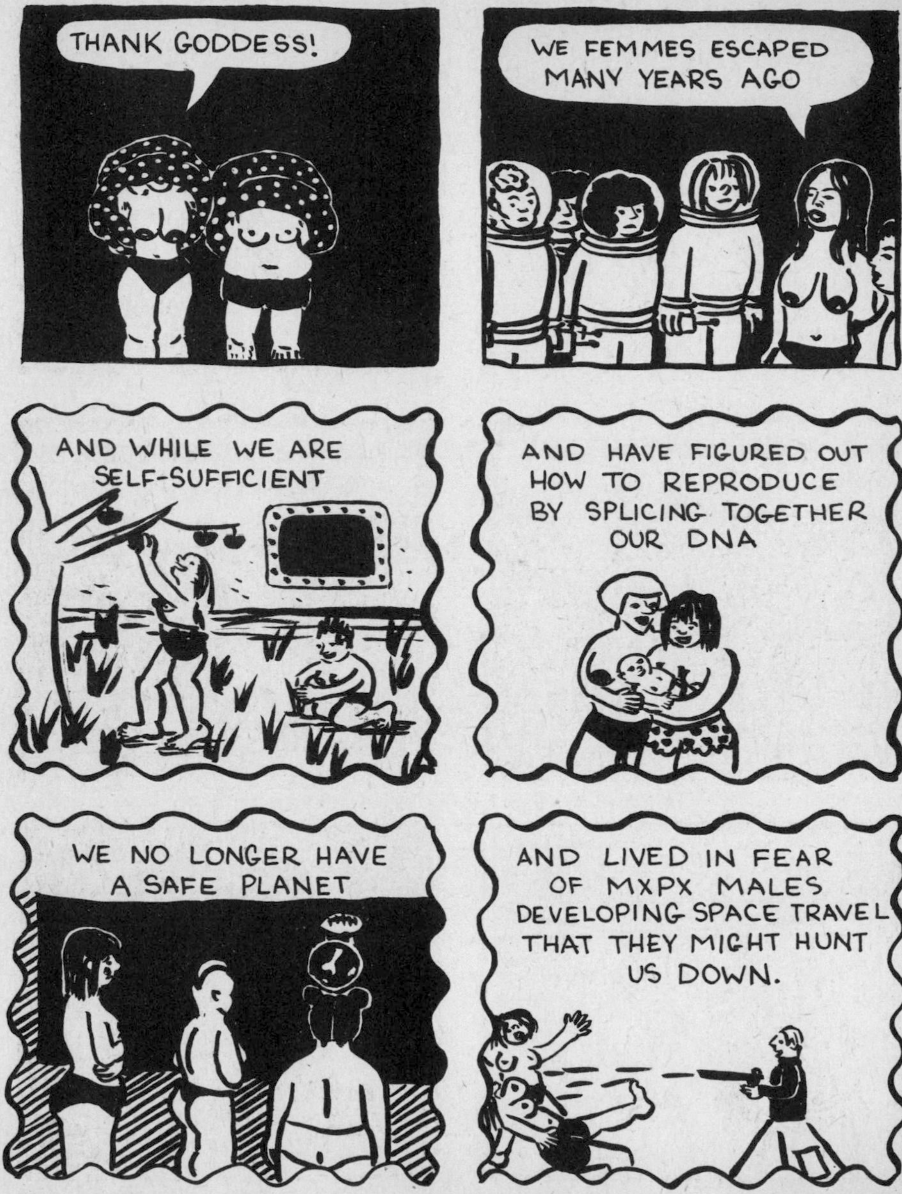

THANK GODDESS!
WE FEMMES ESCAPED MANY YEARS AGO
AND WHILE WE ARE SELF-SUFFICIENT
AND HAVE FIGURED OUT HOW TO REPRODUCE BY SPLICING TOGETHER OUR DNA
WE NO LONGER HAVE A SAFE PLANET
AND LIVED IN FEAR OF MXPX MALES DEVELOPING SPACE TRAVEL THAT THEY MIGHT HUNT US DOWN.

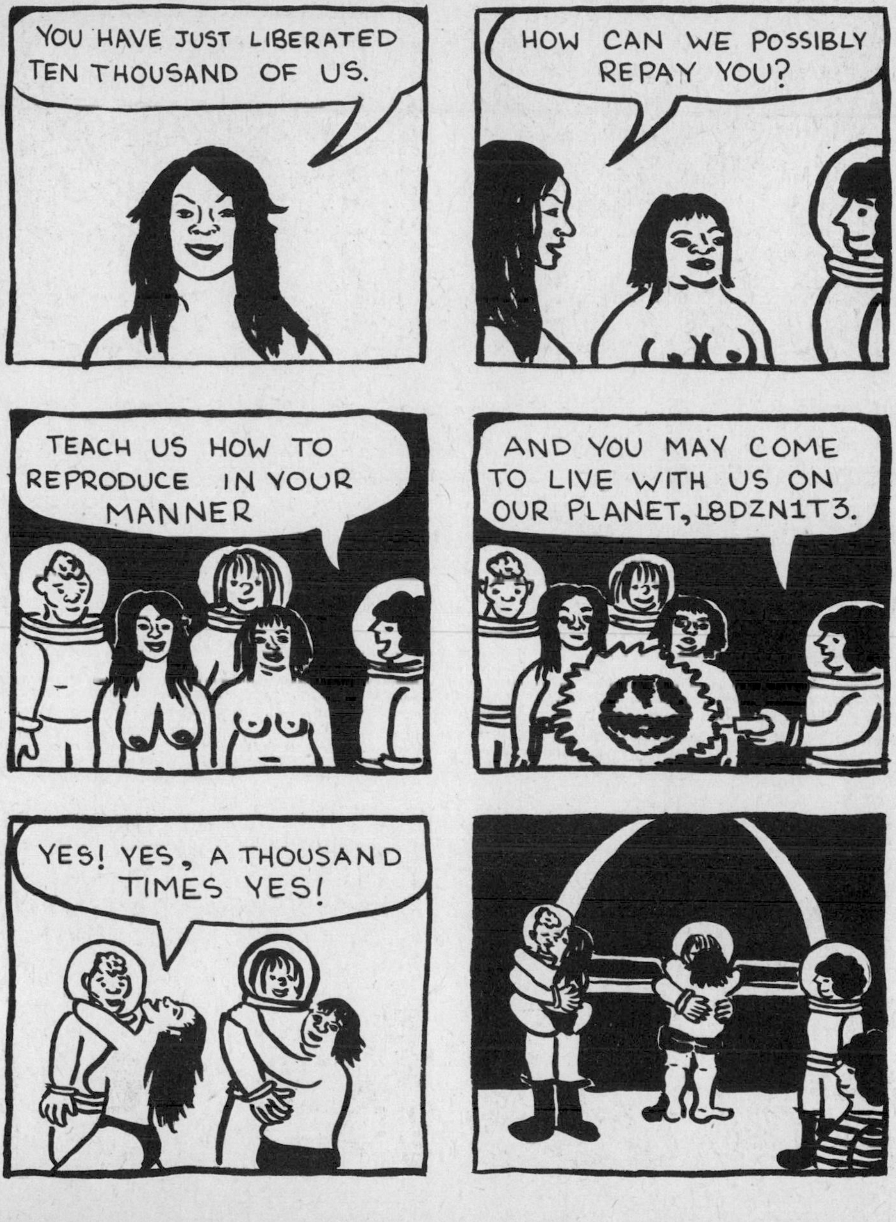
YOU HAVE JUST LIBERATED TEN THOUSAND OF US.
HOW CAN WE POSSIBLY REPAY YOU?
TEACH US HOW TO REPRODUCE IN YOUR MANNER
AND YOU MAY COME TO LIVE WITH US ON OUR PLANET, L8DZN1T3.
YES! YES, A THOUSAND TIMES YES!

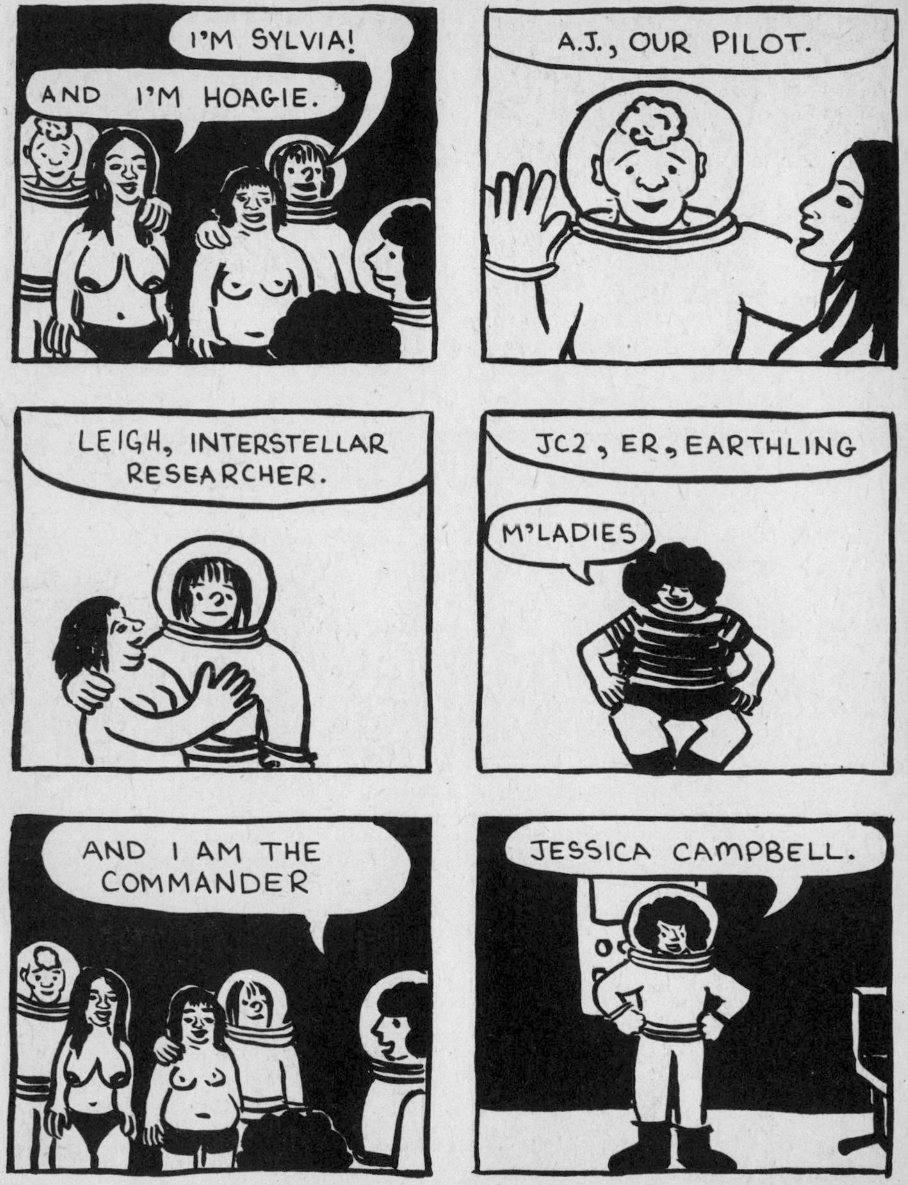
I'M SYLVIA!
AND I'M HOAGIE.
A.J., OUR PILOT.
LEIGH, INTERSTELLAR RESEARCHER.
JC2, ER, EARTHLING
M'LADIES
AND I AM THE COMMANDER
JESSICA CAMPBELL.

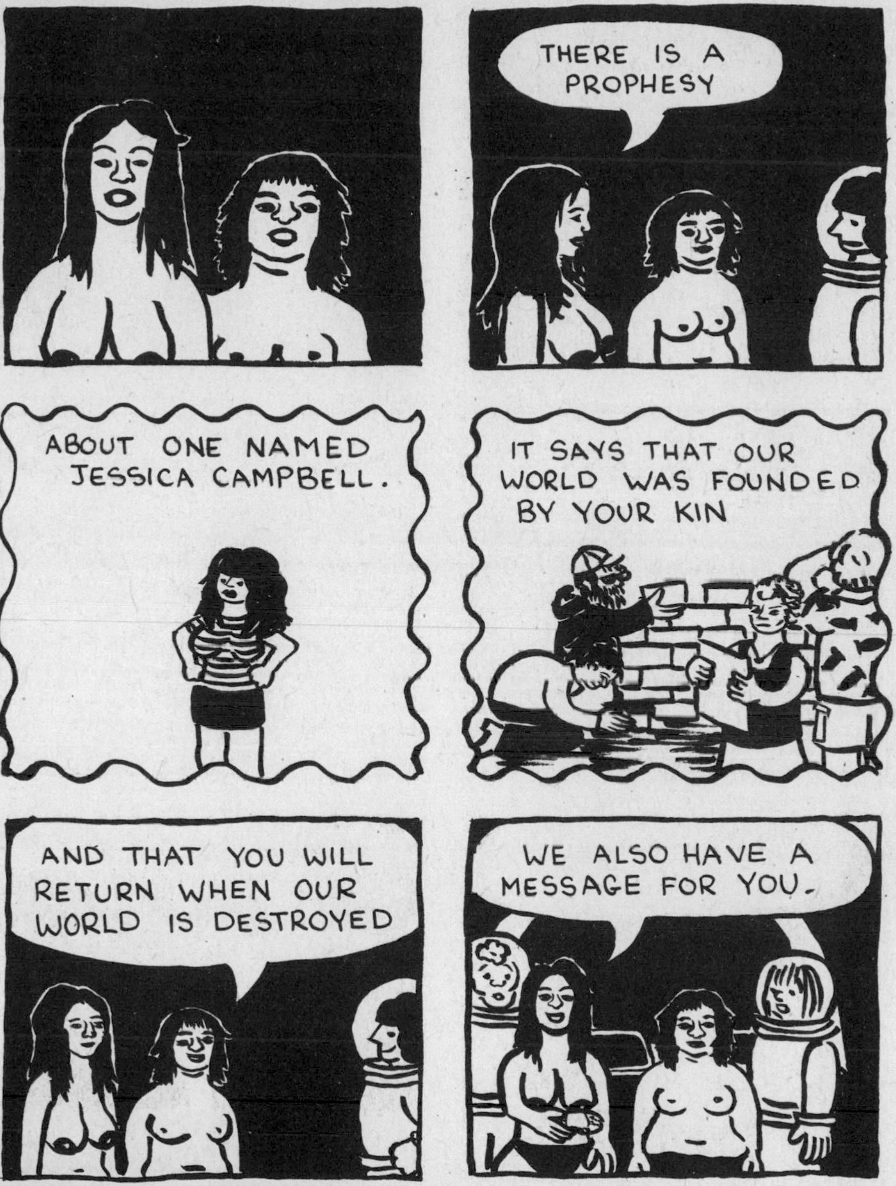
THERE IS A PROPHESY
ABOUT ONE NAMED JESSICA CAMPBELL.
IT SAYS THAT OUR WORLD WAS FOUNDED BY YOUR KIN
AND THAT YOU WILL RETURN WHEN OUR WORLD IS DESTROYED
WE ALSO HAVE A MESSAGE FOR YOU.

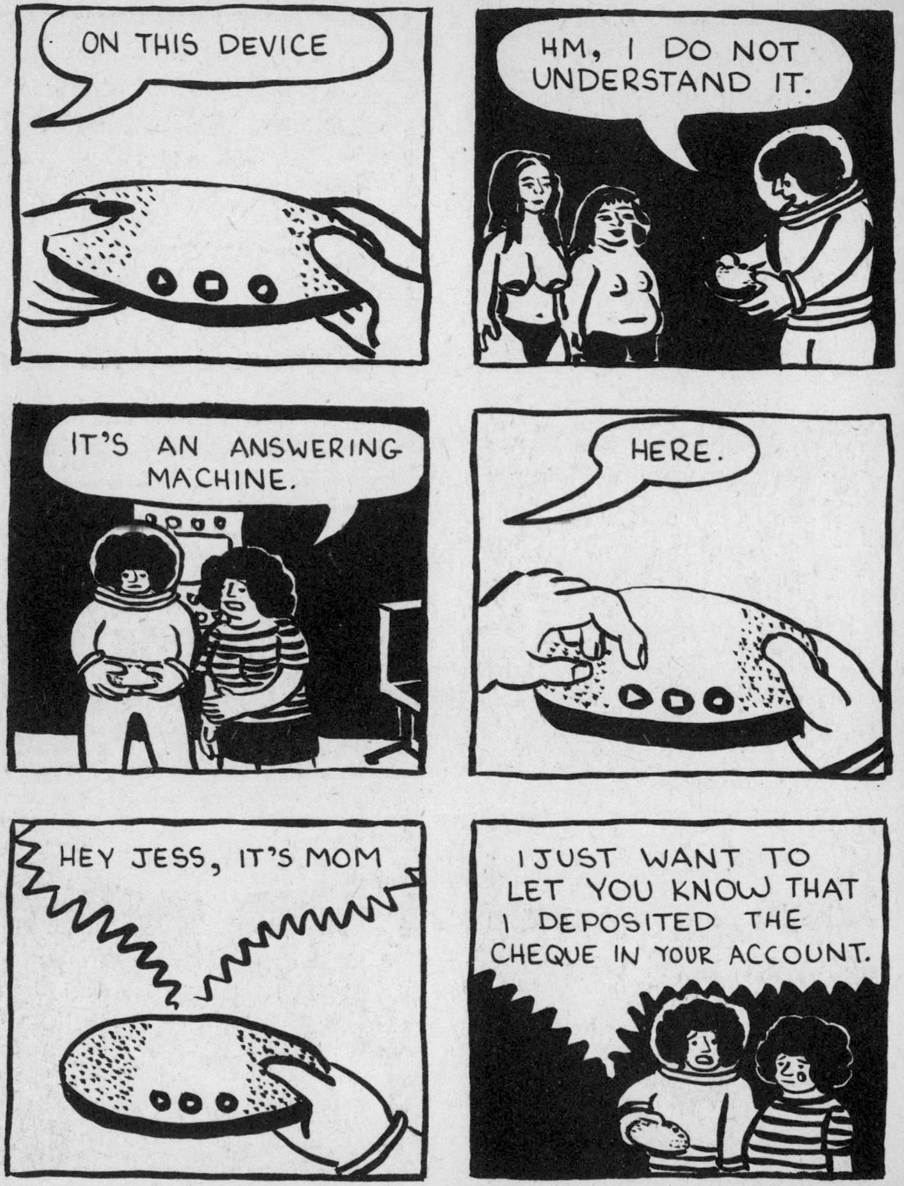
ON THIS DEVICE
HM, I DO NOT UNDERSTAND IT.
IT'S AN ANSWERING MACHINE.
HERE.
HEY JESS, IT'S MOM
I JUST WANT TO LET YOU KNOW THAT I DEPOSITED THE CHEQUE IN YOUR ACCOUNT.

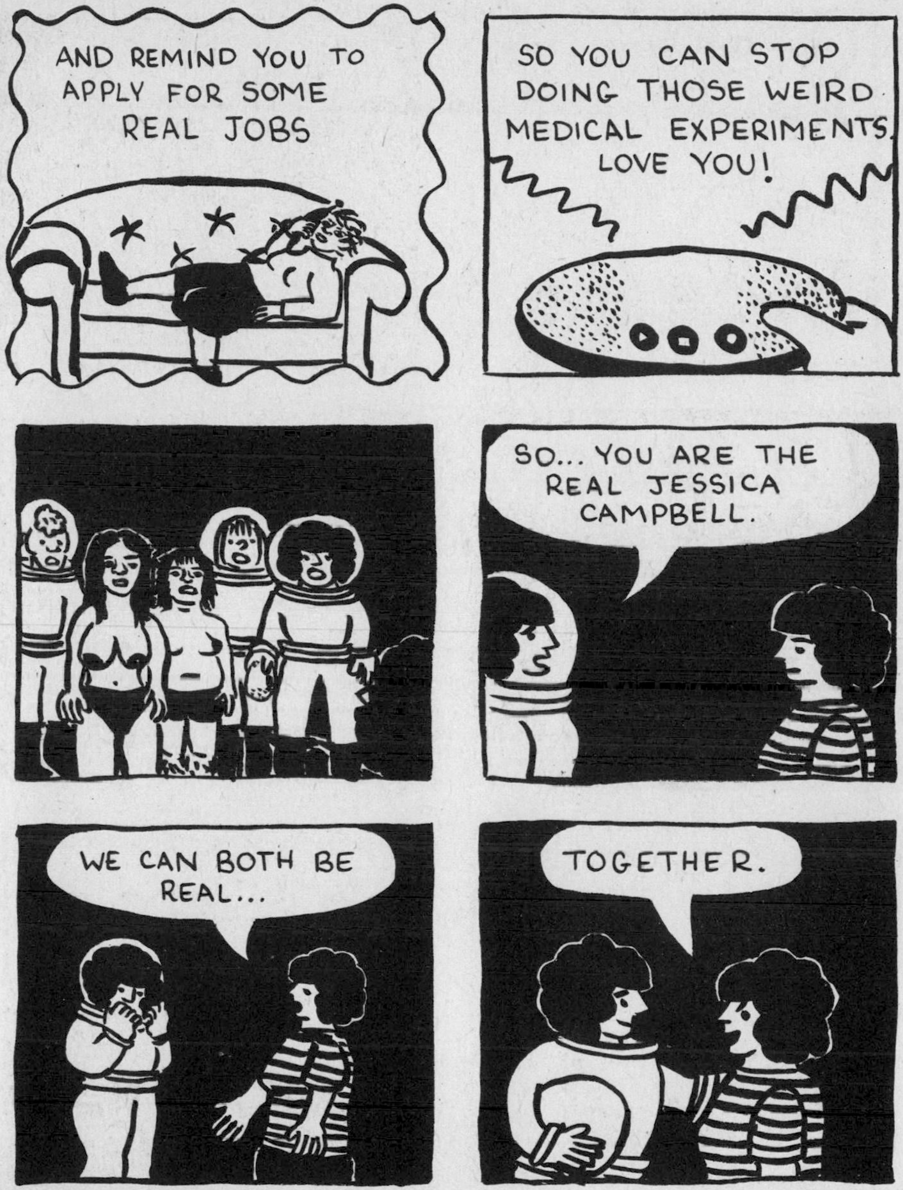
AND REMIND YOU TO APPLY FOR SOME REAL JOBS
SO YOU CAN STOP DOING THOSE WEIRD MEDICAL EXPERIMENTS. LOVE YOU!
SO... YOU ARE THE REAL JESSICA CAMPBELL.
WE CAN BOTH BE REAL...
TOGETHER.

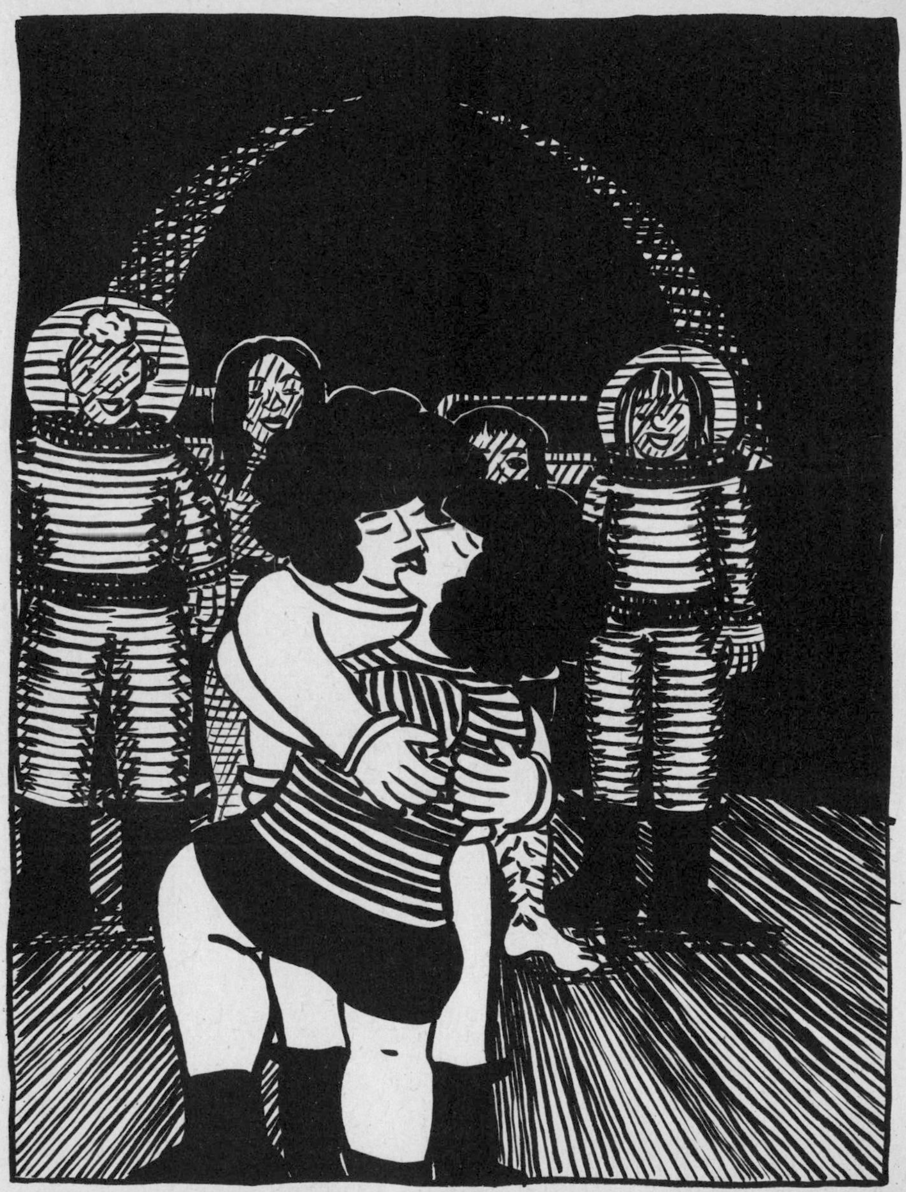

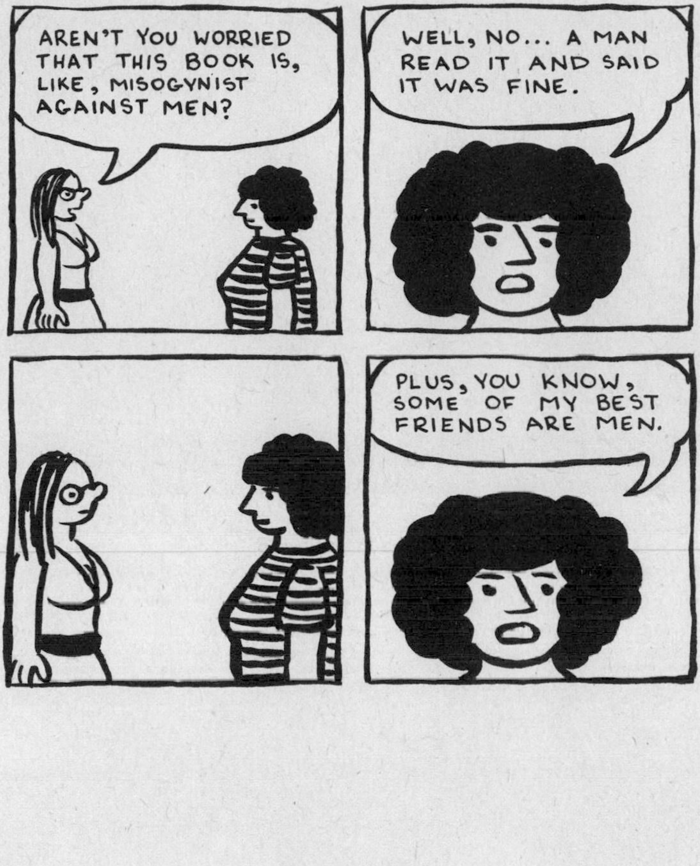
AREN'T YOU WORRIED THAT THIS BOOK IS, LIKE, MISOGYNIST AGAINST MEN?
WELL, NO... A MAN READ IT AND SAID IT WAS FINE.
PLUS, YOU KNOW, SOME OF MY BEST FRIENDS ARE MEN.

ENORMOUS GRATITUDE TO AARON RENIER, ALISON FORGAY, RORY CAMPBELL, TAYLOR CAMPBELL, EM KETTNER, BRIDGET MOSER, TRACY HURREN, ALISON NATURALE, ANYA DAVIDSON, EMMA ALLEN, CLAIRE BOUCHER, ED KANERVA AND, OF COURSE, ANNE KOYAMA.

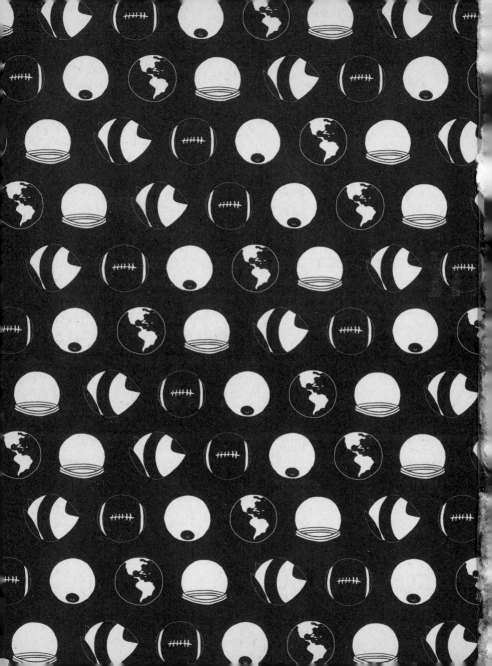